Silent Stars SPEAK

A Fun Sticker and Activity Book

Keith McCullough

DayOne

© Day One Publications 2011

Scripture quotations are from The New International Version unless otherwise stated.
©1973, 1978, 1984, International Bible Society. Published by Hodder and Stoughton.

All space photographs are in the public domain and are published courtesy of one or more of the following:
NASA
European Space Agency (ESA)
Space Telescope Science Institute

Photo of the total eclipse on page 46 is published courtesy of NASA/JPL-Caltech.

British Library Cataloguing in Publication Data available
ISBN 978-1-84625-291-4

Published by Day One Publications
Ryelands Road, Leominster, HR6 8NZ
TEL 01568 613 740   FAX 01568 611 473
email—sales@dayone.co.uk
web site—www.dayone.co.uk
North American e-mail—usasales@dayone.co.uk
North American web site—www.dayonebookstore.com

All rights reserved

No part of this publication may be reproduced, or stored in a retrieval system, or transmitted, in any form or by any means, mechanical, electronic, photocopying, recording or otherwise, without the prior permission of Day One Publications.

Cover design by Wayne McMaster
Internal page design by Caroline McCausland

Printed by Orchard Press Cheltenham Ltd.

Contents

	A Word from the Author 4
	Introduction 5
Lesson 1	In the Beginning 6
Lesson 2	Each One is Special 10
Lesson 3	N.S.E.W. 14
Lesson 4	The Signpost 18
Lesson 5	More Constellations 22
Lesson 6	The Dog Star................. 26
Lesson 7	The Planets: Earth............ 30
Lesson 8	The Planets: Venus 34
Lesson 9	The Solar System............. 38
Lesson 10	Comets and Shooting Stars...... 42
Lesson 11	Eclipse of the Sun 46
Lesson 12	The Christmas Star........... 50
	Answers to Activities 54
	About the Author 64

A Word from the Author

The sky at night is a visual aid to the glory of God. Just as there are billions of people on the face of the earth and each one is special in God's sight, so there are countless billions of stars in the heavens, and each is unique. Stars in the heavens and people on earth alike declare the creative power of God, and all are called to praise His name. So we lift up our eyes in wonder, love and worship.

In down-to-earth terms, I suggest that you go out and buy a Planeshere (star road map), contact your local astronomical society, go along to the next stargazing night and enjoy what you find out!

Introduction

The more we understand the wonders of God's creation, in particular how enormous and beautiful the cosmos is, the more we appreciate how great our God is. So science and faith complement each other. Indeed, someone once said that 'a scientist is someone who thinks God's thoughts after Him.' This was certainly true of the great physicist and astronomer, Isaac Newton, a man who venerated the biblical account of creation and who discovered God's law of gravity, which holds the whole universe together.

Why is the universe so awe-inspiring? Because it reflects the majesty of God on the one hand and on the other puts man in his place. 'What is man?' asks the Psalmist. Man's whole history has been carried out on just one tiny speck in the vast regions of space. Yet God's glory is magnified because He cared so much about that tiny speck that He visited it and died for it in the person of the Saviour, the Lord Jesus Christ.

Stickers
The stickers that accompany this book are for peeling off and placing over the matching pictures that are ghosted out throughout the lessons.

1 Silent Stars Speak
In the Beginning

The night was cold and crystal clear. The sky was ablaze with stars.

What were they saying? What were they singing? Psalm 19 gives the answer.

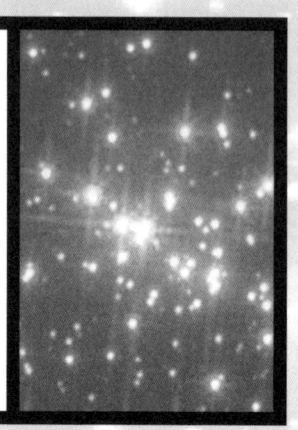

1. *Unscramble the letters to find out what Psalm 19:1 says.*

The _____ declare the _____ of God.
     NAHVESE   **LYROG**

Have you ever stepped out of doors on a dark, clear night and gazed at the stars?

If it's dark enough and away from the street lights' glare, you can see hundreds of them.

The sky is not empty at all. It is full of little lights besides stars.

2. Name the following things that fill the sky.

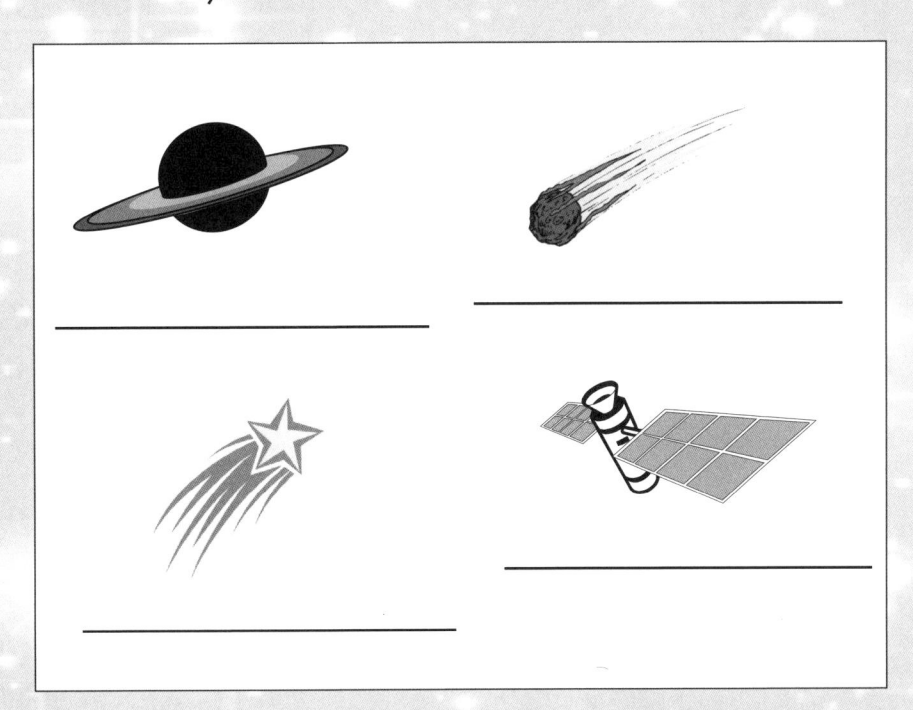

_____   _____

_____   _____

All of these are hanging in space.

Some planets are bigger than our sun, but they are so far away they look like tiny specks.

7

Where did all these lights come from?

Some people say there was a BIG BANG, like a giant firework exploding, and stars were shot out into space.

The Bible says God made them. He flung them into space.

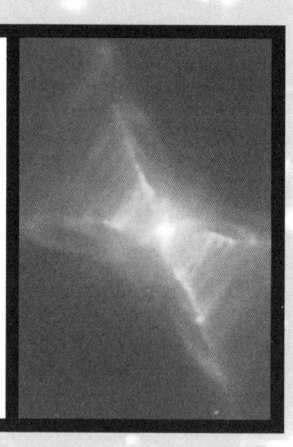

3. Use the code below to complete the sentence.

A	B	C	D	E	F	G	H	I	J	K	L	M
1	2	3	4	5	6	7	8	9	10	11	12	13
N	O	P	Q	R	S	T	U	V	W	X	Y	Z
14	15	16	17	18	19	20	21	22	23	24	25	26

God is ___ ___ ___   ___ ___ ___ ___ ___ ___ ___ ___.
         1 12 12   16 15 23 5 18 6 21 12

4. Unscramble the letters using Genesis 1:14, 18.

God said, 'Let there be _____ in the sky.'
                        TLSHIG

And God saw that it was _____.
                        OGDO

8

God made the earth and the sky, and then He filled the sky with lights.

5. Read Genesis 1:14-16. Complete the crossword puzzle using what you read and the clues.

DOWN

1. The stars were created to help us figure these out; each of these are made up of 365 days.

2. The lesser light

3. The stars were created to give light on this planet.

ACROSS

4, 5. God created lights to divide or separate the _____ from the _____.

6. One of the functions of stars is to help us tell the four of these.

2 Silent Stars Speak
Each One is Special

1. Read Psalm 147:4. What two things beginning with the letter 'n' does God know about the stars?

Their n_____ and their n_____

2. Fill in the blanks with the opposite of each word in brackets.

Each star is _____ (the same).

Some are _____ (far).

Some are _____ (near).

Some are _____ (white).

Some are blue, red or orange.

Some are _____ (small).

Some are _____ (bigger).

Some are very _____ (cold).

Some are not.

Our nearest STAR is the sun. In fact, all stars are suns, and they all give out light and HEAT.

The sun is 400 times further away from us than the MOON.

So if you climbed a sunbeam, it would take you three THOUSAND six hundred years to get there.

The sun is also 400 times BIGGER than the moon. So from Earth they both look the same SIZE.

God has given us the sun to give us LIGHT and WARMTH.

All our life and ENERGY come from the sun.

If we were any nearer to the sun, we would BURN up. If we were any further away from the sun, we would freeze.

We are just the right DISTANCE away.

God is GOOD.

3. Find all the words in CAPITALS in the boxes above and write them here:

_____

_____

4. Look for the words in capitals you wrote down on the previous page in the letter grid below and colour them in. The words may be up, down, diagonal or backwards.

I	Q	T	J	R	I	X	S	Q	E	X	S	A	J	T	Q
X	O	Z	E	N	E	R	G	Y	N	E	J	E	Q	N	H
J	D	O	S	J	F	X	T	J	H	X	E	H	L	X	E
E	A	Q	V	T	Q	B	Q	E	J	N	S	A	I	J	A
N	D	X	M	Q	A	U	J	A	Q	K	E	X	G	S	T
D	I	T	T	S	J	R	C	W	A	R	M	T	H	I	R
I	X	C	H	U	I	N	Q	T	J	Z	T	O	T	J	Q
S	T	H	J	O	E	J	O	T	M	O	O	N	H	Q	E
T	R	Z	Q	N	U	X	O	Q	Z	T	X	H	I	X	N
A	Q	G	S	J	I	S	D	J	S	Z	H	J	Q	J	I
N	D	J	I	D	X	O	A	E	N	X	F	Z	R	O	X
C	M	Q	Z	I	O	X	T	N	S	H	E	Q	A	T	P
E	S	A	E	G	Q	L	Q	M	D	R	E	G	G	I	B

5. Colour in all boxes with the letters J, Q, X and Z in the letter grid.

6. Write the letters left over on the blanks below from left to right to read a Bible verse about the sun.

__ __ __ __ __ __ __ __ __ __ __ __

__ __ __ __ __ __ __ __

__ __ __ __ __ __ __ __ __ __

__ __ __ __ __ __ __ __ __ __ __ __ __

__ __ __ __ __ __ __ __ __ __ __ __;

__ __ __ __ __ __ __ __ __ __ __ __ __

__ __ __ __ __ __ __ __ __ __ __.

__ __ __ __ __ __ 19:6

Our nearest neighbour in the sky is the moon.

It's very near compared to the stars. In fact, men have visited the moon and walked on its surface.

7. Use the code below to complete the sentences.

A	B	C	D	E	F	G	H	I	J	K	L	M

N	O	P	Q	R	S	T	U	V	W	X	Y	Z

If you could walk up a __m__ __o__ __o__ __n__ __b__ __e__ __a__ __m__

at the same rate that you walk to school, you could get there in just __n__ __i__ __n__ __e__ years.

The moon has no light of its own, but it reflects the __s__ __u__ __n__ __l__ __i__ __g__ __h__ __t__ like a mirror.

Neil Armstrong was the first man to step onto the moon. When he did so, he said: *'That's one small step for man, one giant leap for mankind.'*

3 Silent Stars Speak
N.S.E.W.

1. *Unscramble the letters to spell one of the four directions—North, South, East or West.*

The sun rises in the _____.
SATE

If you look in the direction of the sunrise, you are looking East.

The sun sets in the _____,
TWSE
which is on the opposite side of the sky.

If your house faces East and West, you can watch the sun rise in the morning and then set in the evening.

At midday the sun is halfway between the East and West, and we call that _____ (unless you live in Australia!).
TOSUH

Opposite the South is the _____.
ORHTN

We can divide the sky up into four quarters like a sponge cake, and we call the quarters the N.S.E.W. parts of the sky.

Of course, the sun doesn't really rise and set at all. It stays where it is.

It's our little world that spins round like a top toward the sun.

It spins at a thousand miles an hour from West to East.

You can't feel it spinning because the air spins with it.

So in the morning, one side of the world faces the sun and in the evening, the other side of the world faces the sun.

So every hour of the day, people are waking up to a new day and there is always somebody praising God.

2. Answer the following questions:

On what side of the earth are you right now—the dark or the light side? _____

On what side of the earth are you when you sleep at night? _____

What would somebody on the other side of the world be doing when you are getting ready to go to bed?

_____

3. Read this poem out loud:

> Across each continent and island
> As dawn leads on another day,
> The voice of prayer is never silent,
> Nor dies the sound of praise away.
>
> –from 'The day thou gavest'
> by John Ellerton

5. According to this poem, what are people doing somewhere on earth all the time?

_____

4. Find Psalm 113:3 and fill in the missing blanks from it:

'From the rising of the _____ to the place where it sets, the name of the _____ is to be praised.'

5. Follow these instructions.

Put the four directions in order so that the first letter of each reads GOOD ___ ___ ___ ___. (For a clue, you will find the words in Luke 2:10).

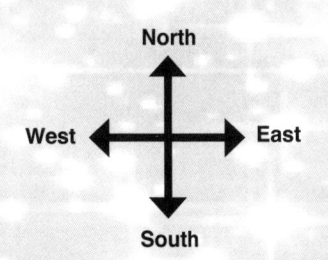

5. Circle the right answer. The answers are on this activity sheet.

How fast does the Earth spin each hour?
- A. ten miles each hour
- B. hundred miles each hour
- C. thousand miles each hour
- D. million miles each hour

In what direction does the Earth spin?
- A. North to South
- B. West to East
- C. South to North
- D. East to West

In what direction does the sun set?
- A. North
- B. South
- C. East
- D. West

17

4 Silent Stars Speak
The Signpost

The stars are arranged in groups called constellations. These make pictures in the sky.

If you turn your back on the South and look towards the North, you will see, high in the sky, a constellation called the Plough, or the Big Dipper or even the Saucepan.

This is because if you join up the seven stars, you get a picture like a plough or pan.

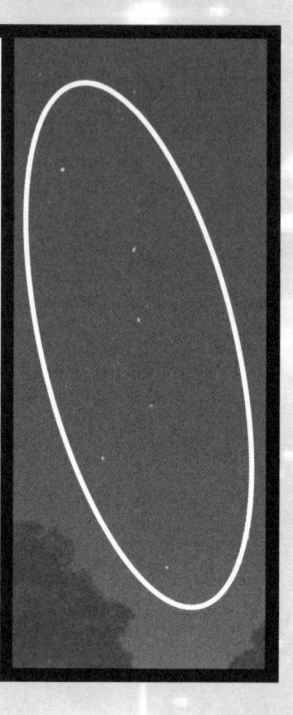

1. *Join up the stars to see the shape of the Plough constellation.*

```
              2*
1*          3*
                    4*8                    7*


                              5*      6*
```

→ (This way to the North Pole!)

2. Use the code below to complete the sentences.

A	B	C	D	E	F	G	H	I	J	K	L	M
1	2	3	4	5	6	7	8	9	10	11	12	13
N	O	P	Q	R	S	T	U	V	W	X	Y	Z
14	15	16	17	18	19	20	21	22	23	24	25	26

Stars numbers 6 and 7 point to the Pole star called

___ ___ ___ ___ ___ ___ ___.
16 15 12 1 18 9 19

Sailors at sea and some ___ ___ ___ ___ ___ on migration find their way by this star.
2 9 18 4 19

Over one ___ ___ ___ ___, the Plough will revolve full circle
25 5 1 18

around this star, but 6 and 7 will always point to it.

Polaris is the one point in the sky which is fixed so you can always find ___ ___ ___ ___ ___.
14 15 18 20 8

In the old days, sailors would steer their ___ ___ ___ ___ ___
                                            19 8   9 16 19

by looking at the stars and not get ___ ___ ___ ___.
                                    12 15 19 20

___ ___ ___ ___ ___ is at the centre of our universe, and
10 5 19 21 19

he holds everything together: 'In ___ ___ ___ all things hold
together.' (Colossians 1:17)   8   9 13

3. Can you find the Plough in the picture below?

4. In what direction would North be if you were looking up at the sky like this? Draw an arrow pointing in the direction of North.

5. See if you can find Polaris in this picture.

6. Complete the crossword puzzle using the clues.

DOWN

1. Another name for the Plough

3. Sailors used the stars as these so they wouldn't get lost.

4. These people used the stars to find their way at sea.

ACROSS

2. Who is at the centre of our universe?

5. We can use Polaris to find this direction.

6. The Plough revolves around this star.

7. It takes one _____ for the Plough to revolve around the answer to number 6.

5 Silent Stars Speak
More Constellations

Now look toward the South, especially in the early evening in the middle of winter, and you will see another great constellation.

It is called Orion the hunter because it looks like the giant figure of a man complete with belt and sword.

He is supposed to be chasing the Bull, but he never catches him.

The top left-hand star is named Betalgeuse (pronounced beetle-juice). It's a mega star and is the tenth brightest star in the sky.

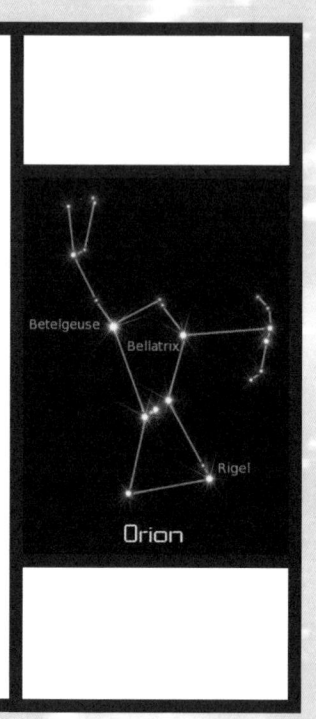

1. Draw a picture of a hunter the way Orion is posed. Don't forget to include the belt and the sword.

But we are more interested in the three stars that make up Orion's belt.

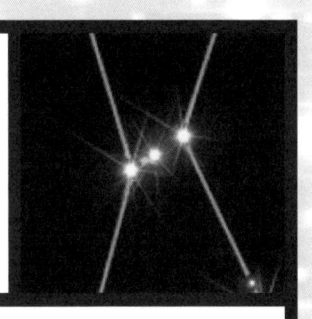

Listen to God speaking to Job: 'Can you loose the belt of Orion?' (Job 38:31b, NKJV)

Job lived a long time ago and he suffered a lot, but he never lost faith in God.

Job knew how weak man was, but he also knew how great God was.

Of course he could not undo Orion's belt, but he knew God could.

Just above the red eye of the Bull, to the right of Orion, is a hazy group of about six stars called the Pleiades.

With binoculars you can see nearly 200 of them.

They are bright and sparkle like precious jewels, making the Pleiades the most beautiful group of stars in the sky.

2. Find and colour the words of Matthew 19:26 on the word grid. The words may be up, down, diagonal or backwards. Colour only one 'with'.

'With man this is impossible; but with God all things are possible.'

Q	Z	G	E	O	F	D	H	K	C	E	V	J	Q
B	K	V	R	A	F	T	J	N	K	L	X	D	O
A	U	F	A	Q	I	H	N	Q	F	B	Y	Z	K
Q	J	T	X	W	J	I	X	T	H	I	N	G	S
V	K	Q	J	V	T	S	K	F	V	S	H	V	Z
F	P	O	S	S	I	B	L	E	Q	S	X	K	F
X	I	V	Q	X	N	J	V	F	K	O	G	J	Z
J	F	S	I	K	V	Q	M	A	N	P	F	V	Q
Q	F	V	Z	F	J	K	J	L	V	M	Z	J	K
K	Z	J	G	O	D	X	F	L	Q	I	K	V	X

3. Colour in all boxes with the letters F, J, K, Q, V, X and Z.

4. From left to right, write out the letters you see on the blanks below. What do they say?

___ ___ ___ ___ ___ ___ ___ ___

___ ___ ___ ___ ___ ___ ___ ___ ___ .

The whole cluster of the Pleiades seems to be enveloped in a faint cloud that binds the stars all together like a net bag full of shiny marbles.

God spoke to Job about this great wonder.

'Can you bind the beautiful Pleiades?' he asked (Job 38:31a).

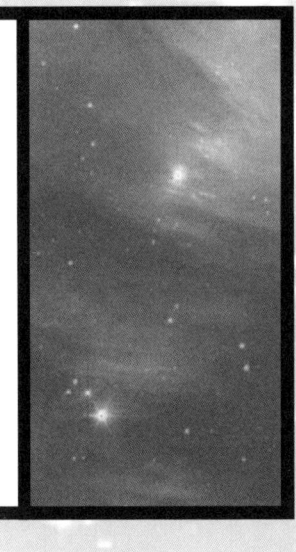

5. Write your name on one of the jewels below. Then colour all the jewels in bright colours.

God wants us to sparkle like jewels.
(Read Zechariah 9:16.)

He wants his children to shine in the universe.
(Read Philippians 2:15.)

He wants to bind us together in love.

6 Silent Stars Speak
The Dog Star

I have a little dog. He walks just behind my left heel.

Orion the hunter has a dog too. He walks just behind Orion's left heel.

The dog's eye is the brightest star in the sky. It's called Sirius.

The little dog follows his master right across the sky just as Jesus wants us to follow him.

Sirius •

1. Find out who uses this star and what they call it. On each blank, write the letter that comes alphabetically before the letter under the blank.

 __ __ __ __ __ __ __ call it the __ __ __
 T B J M P S T   E P H

 __ __ __ __ and use it to guide them home.
 T U B S

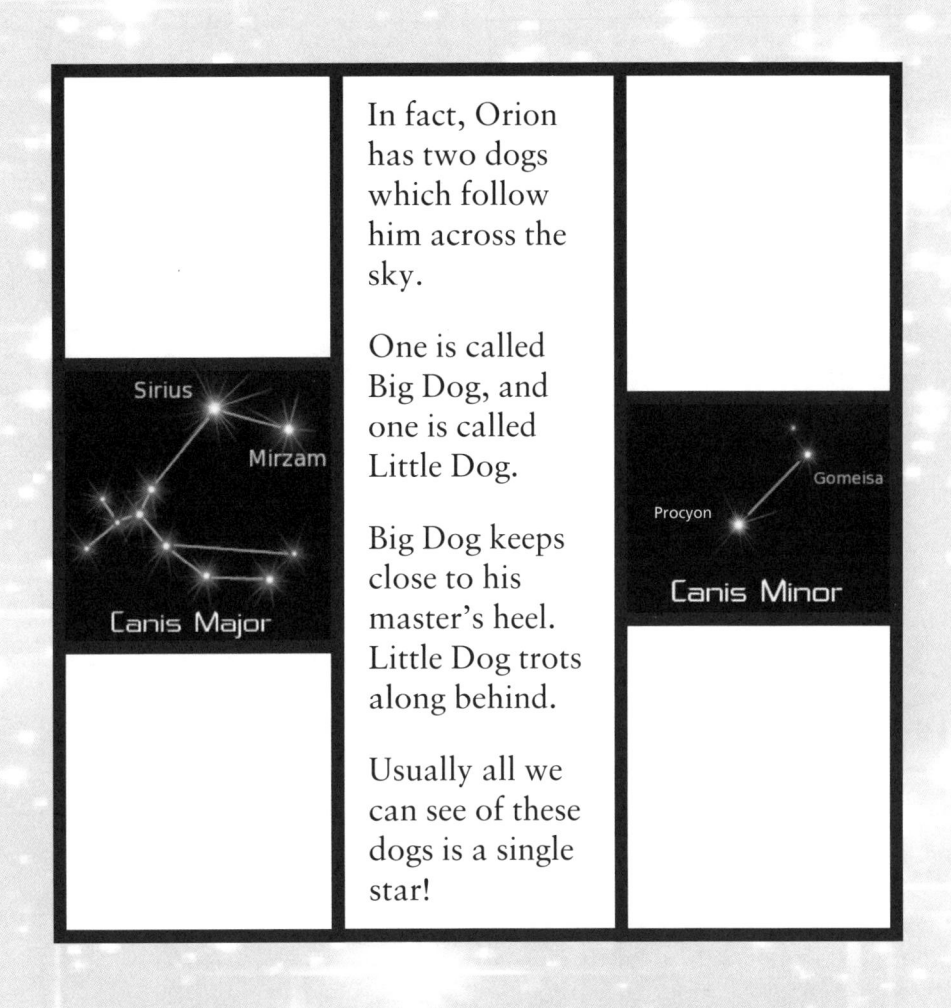

In fact, Orion has two dogs which follow him across the sky.

One is called Big Dog, and one is called Little Dog.

Big Dog keeps close to his master's heel. Little Dog trots along behind.

Usually all we can see of these dogs is a single star!

2. Fill in the blanks below and on the next page with the rest of the words from the list that will fit.

MAJOR　　　MINOR　　　EYE　　　PROCYON

Another name for the Big Dog star is Canis Ma_____r.

Another name for the Little Dog star is Canis Mi_____r.

Little Dog's brightest star is called P_____n.

The part of Little Dog's body that is the brightest in the sky is the _____.

> Betaljeuse, Sirius and Procyon make a bright triangle in the winter sky.

3. Connect the three stars to make a triangle. Then write the name of each star beside the right letter.

*B

*P

*S

4. Complete the crossword puzzle using the clues.

DOWN

2. Little Dog's brightest star

4. Another name for the Dog star

5. The part of Little Dog's body that is the brightest

ACROSS

1. The animal that follows Orion in the sky

3. Another name for the Little Dog constellation is Canis ____.

6. One of the stars that makes a triangle in the sky with Sirius and Procyon

7 Silent Stars Speak
The Planets: Earth

A planet is an object in space that orbits a star.

It is a ball of rock or gas.

It has no light of its own but reflects the star's light.

1. *Unscramble the letters to complete the blanks.*

Our world is a planet. It is called _____.
RATEH

It orbits, or circles around, our star, the _____.
UNS

It reflects the _____ of the sun and looks
GLTIH
beautiful from the moon.

It orbits the sun once every _____, or every 365 days.
AYRE

When the North Pole faces the sun, it is summer in the North.

When the South Pole faces the sun, it is winter in the North.

So when the North is having summer, the South is having winter. When the North is having winter, the South is having summer.

2. Think and answer.

If you lived in Australia and it was summer, what season would it be in each of these parts of the world?

Australia

North America

season: _____

Africa

season: _____

Europe

season: _____

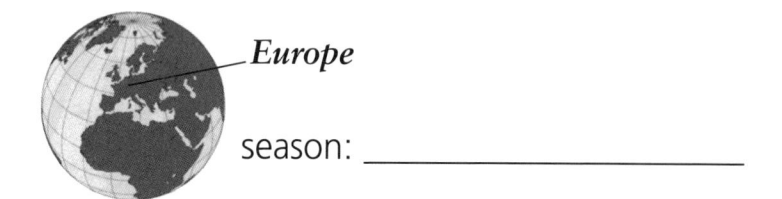

We might think that Earth has a firm foundation and that the sun moves around it.

In the old days, that's what people believed until a famous scientist named Galileo proved them wrong.

3. Fill in the blanks by looking up the Bible references given.

Now we know that Earth moves around in heaven like all the other heavenly bodies.

God's servant Job knew this.

He said that God 'suspends the world on _____' (Job 26:7). Isn't that amazing?

We know a lot about our planet. But is it ours?

The Bible says, 'The _____ is the _____, and everything in it' (Psalm 24:1).

So it doesn't belong to us. It's only ours to look after.

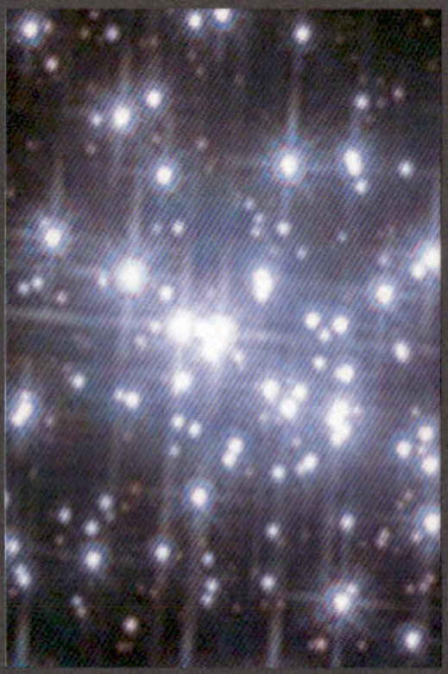
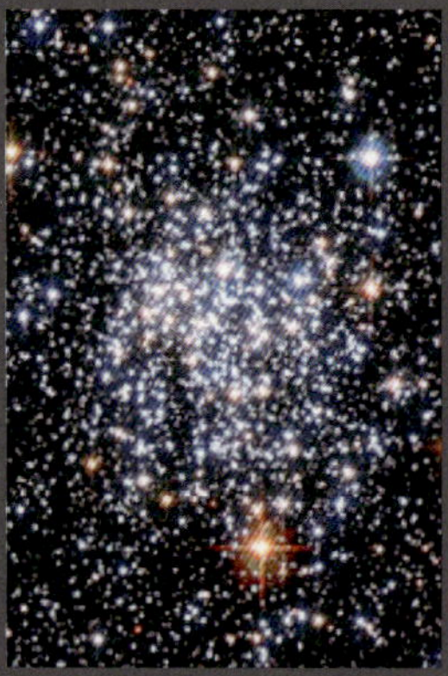
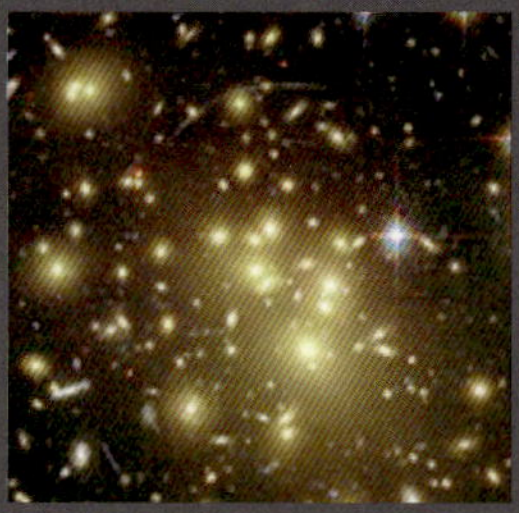
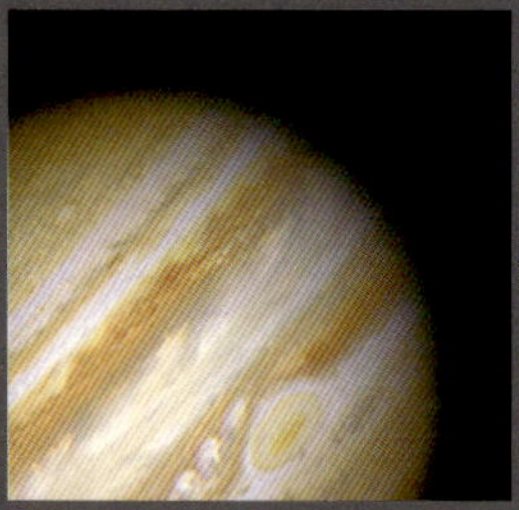
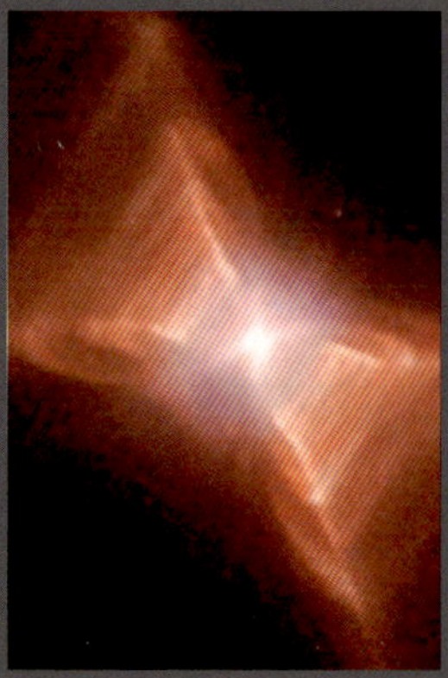
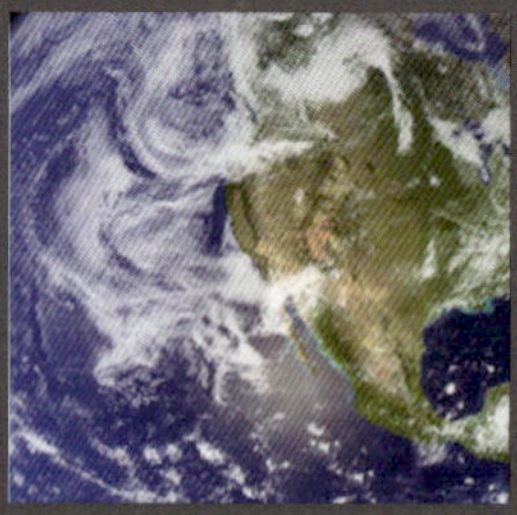
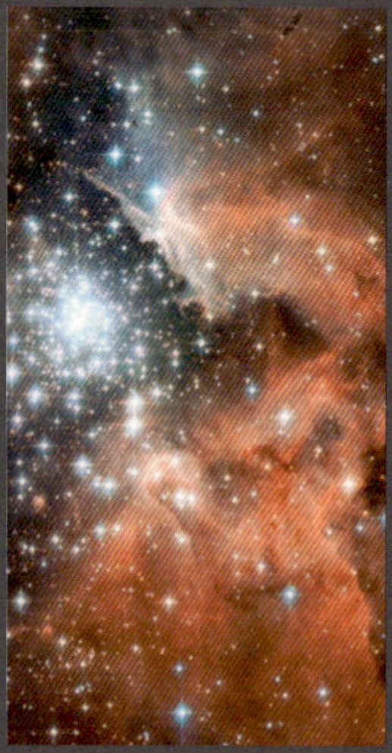
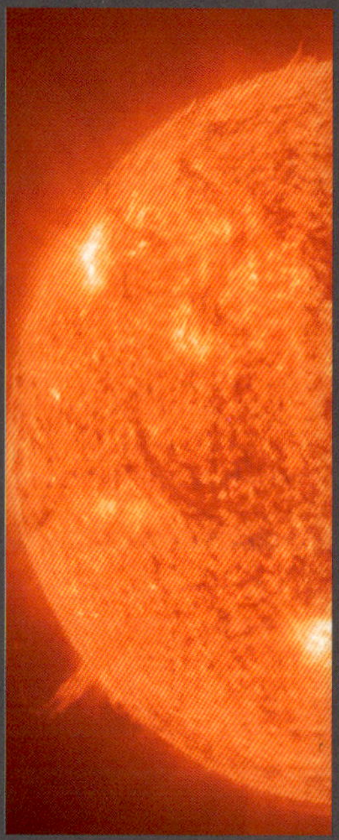
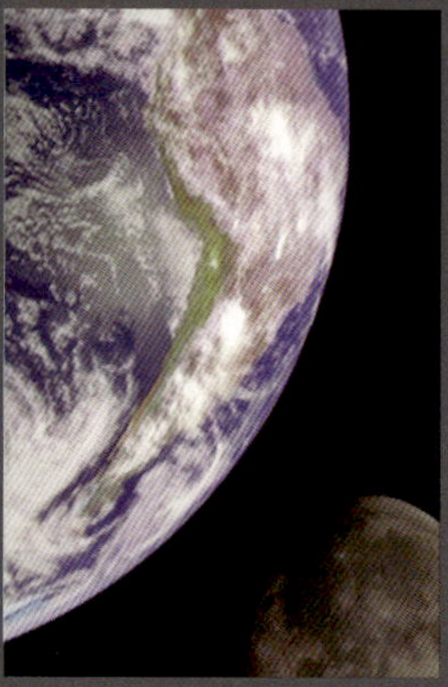
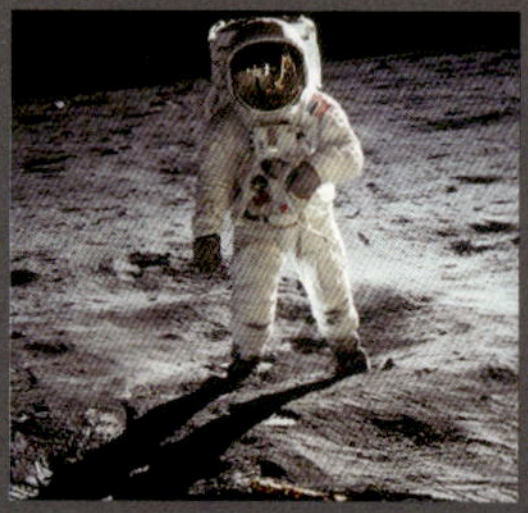
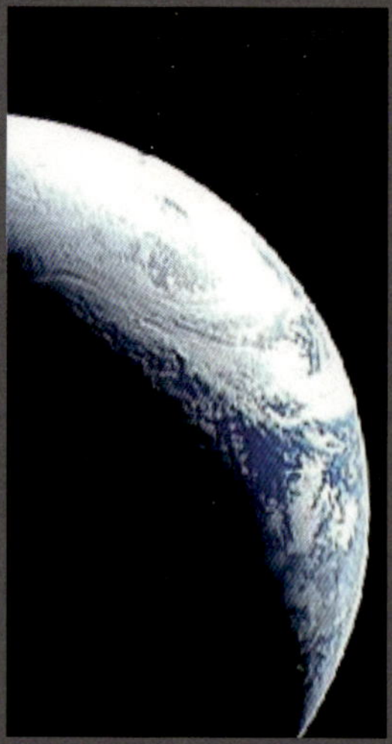
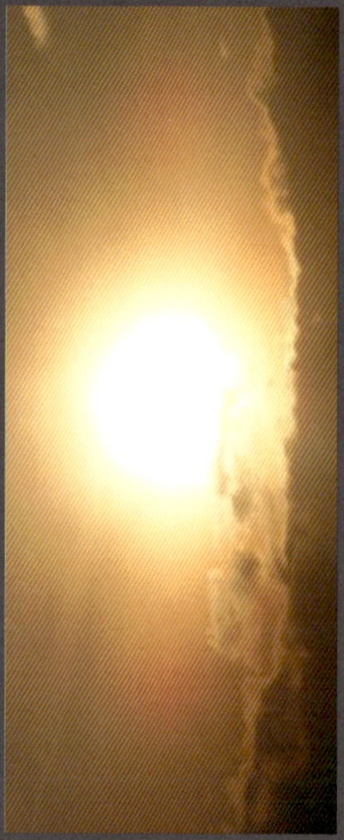
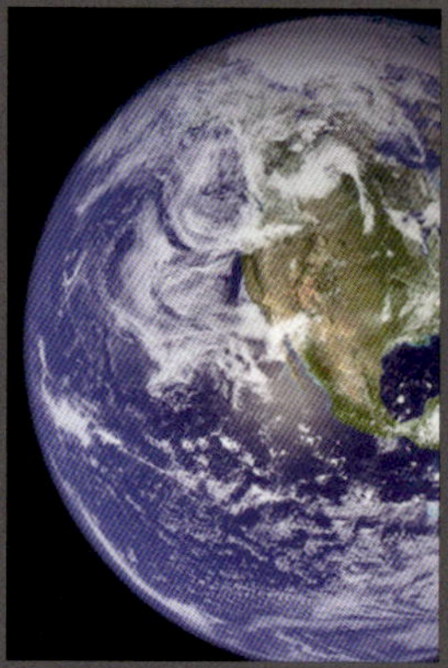

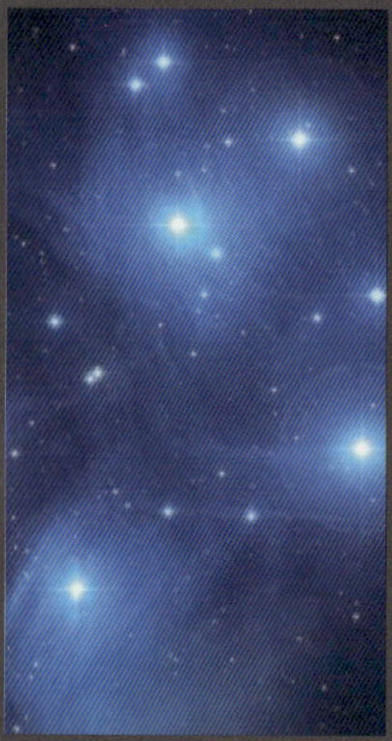
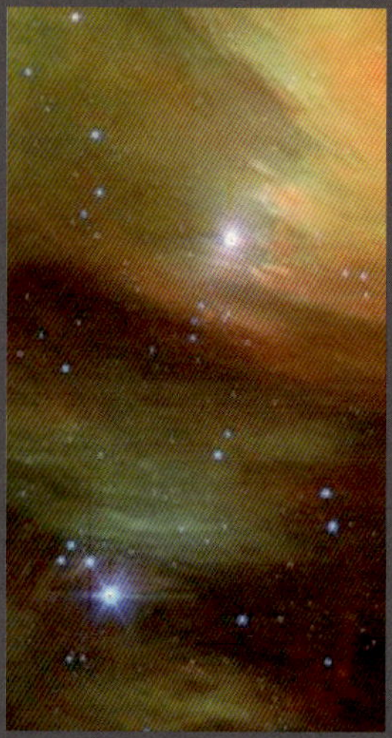
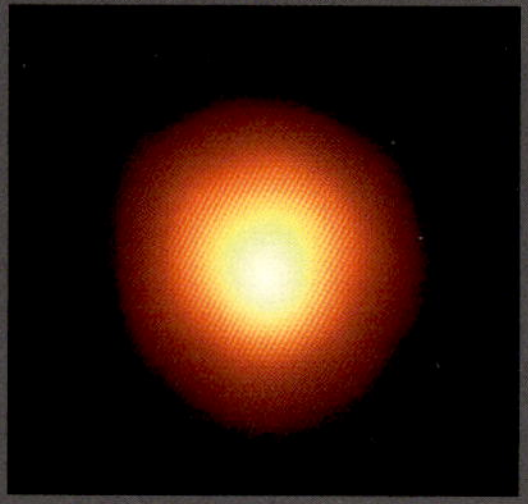

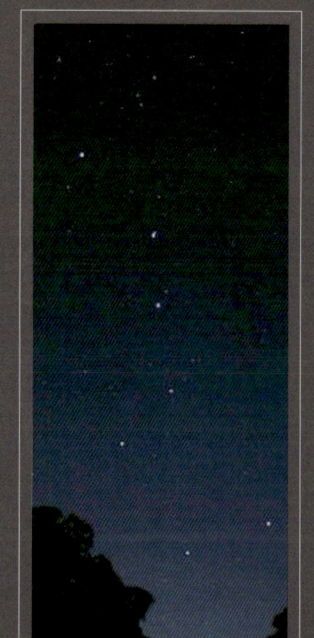

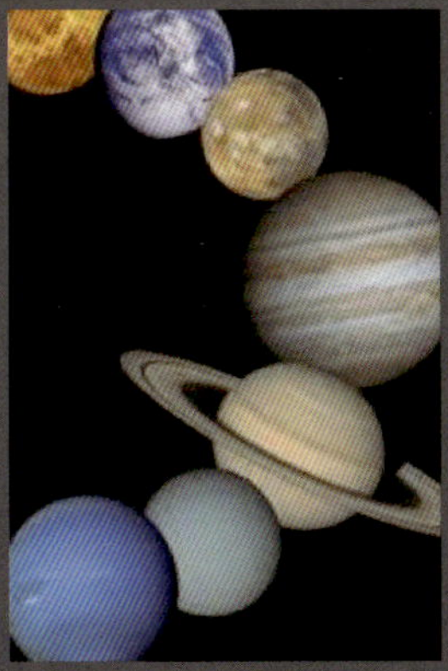
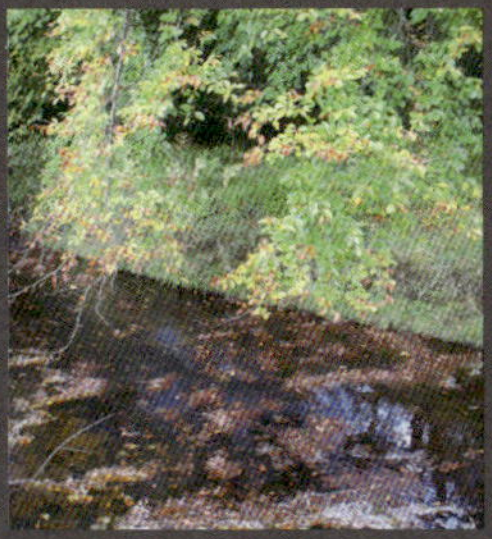
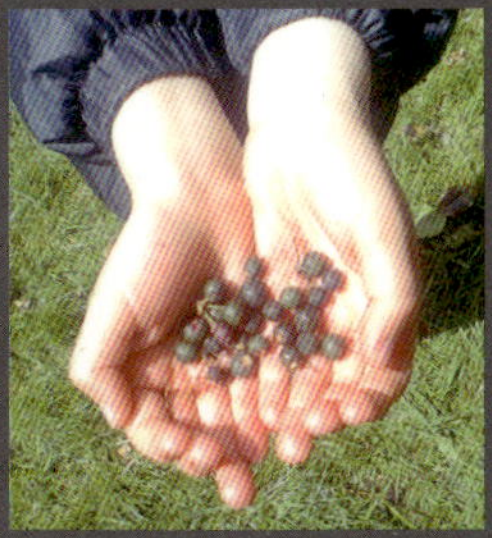

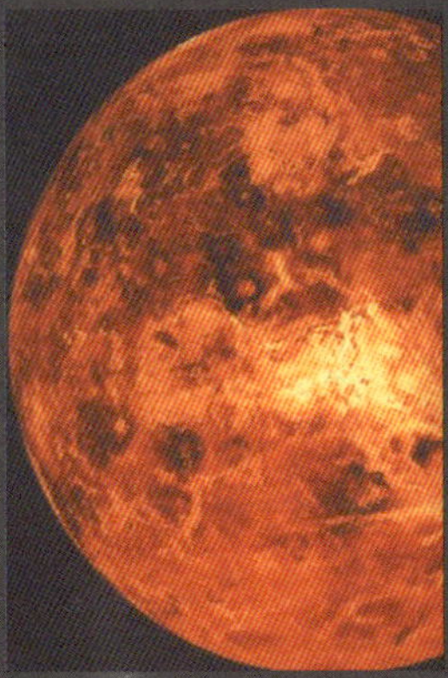
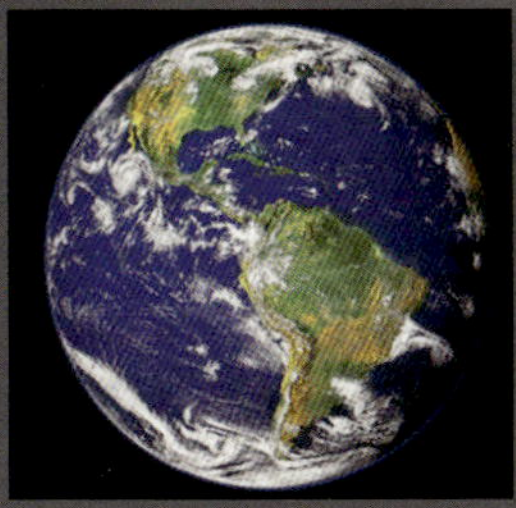
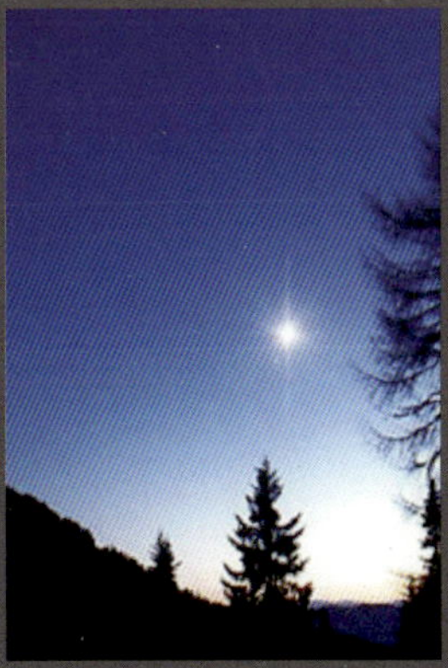
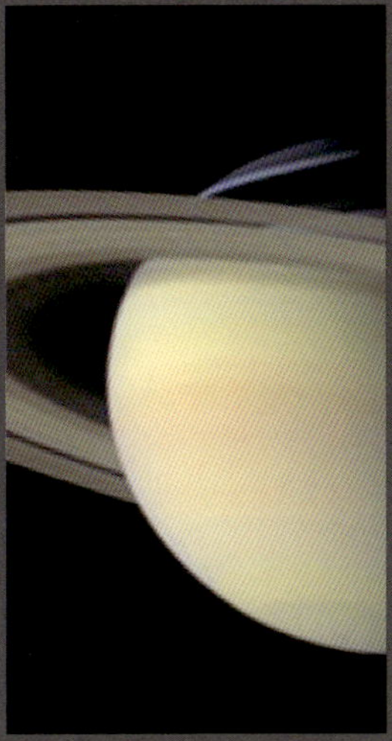
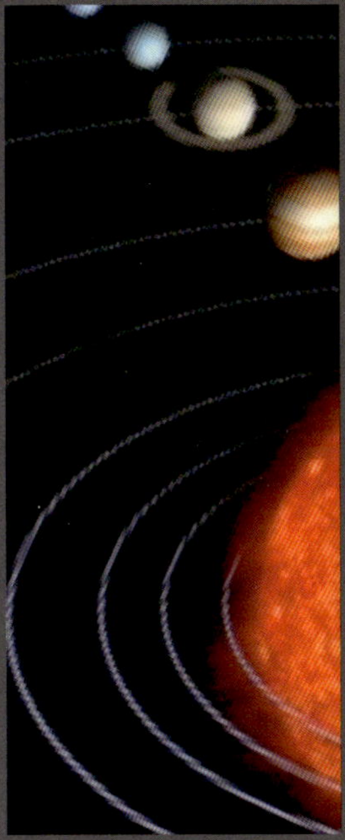
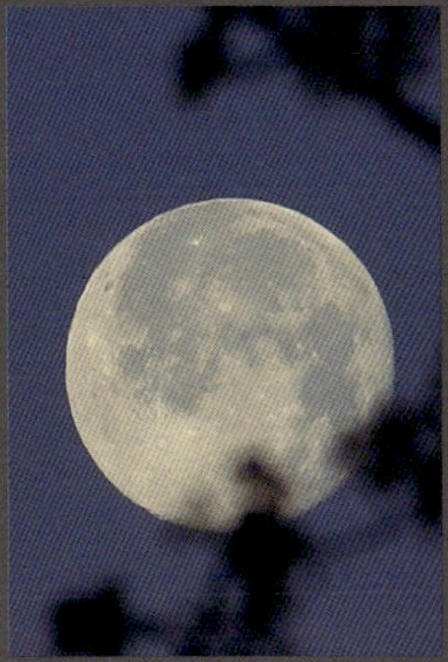
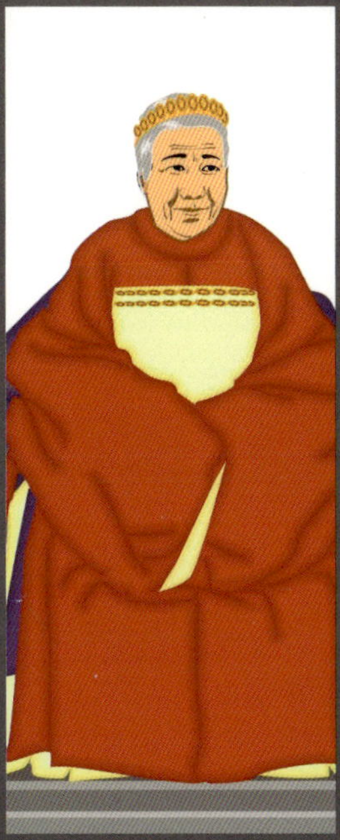
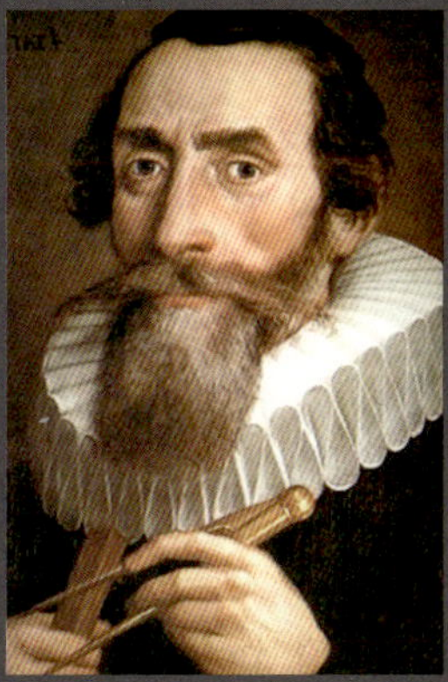
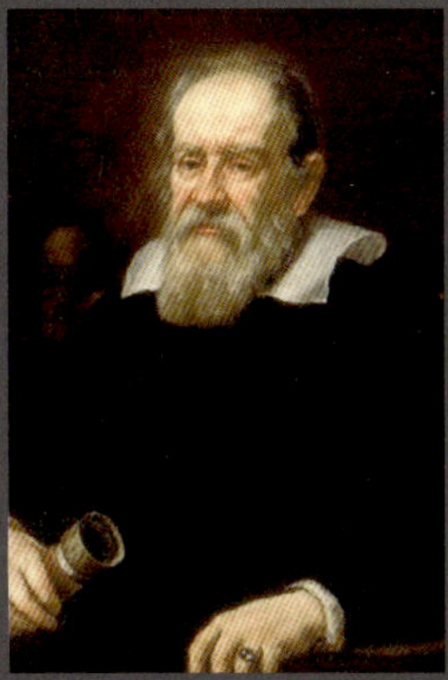
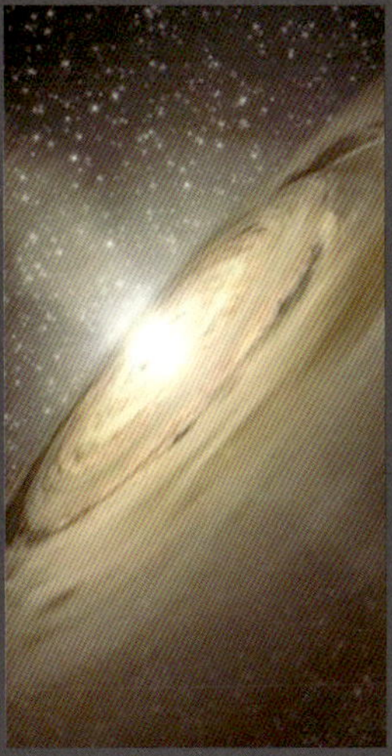
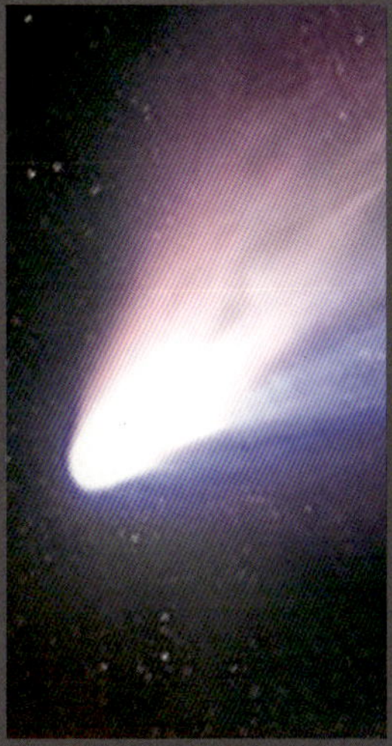
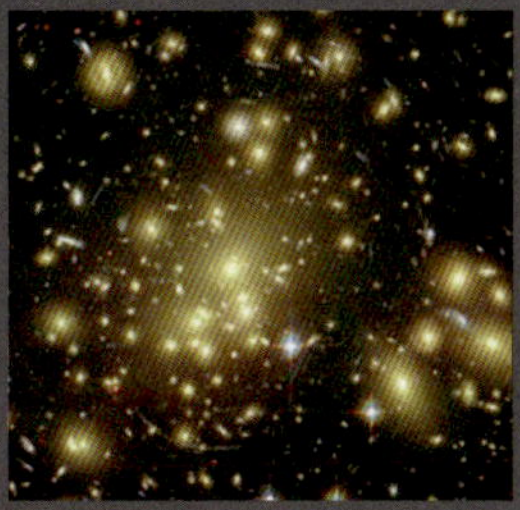
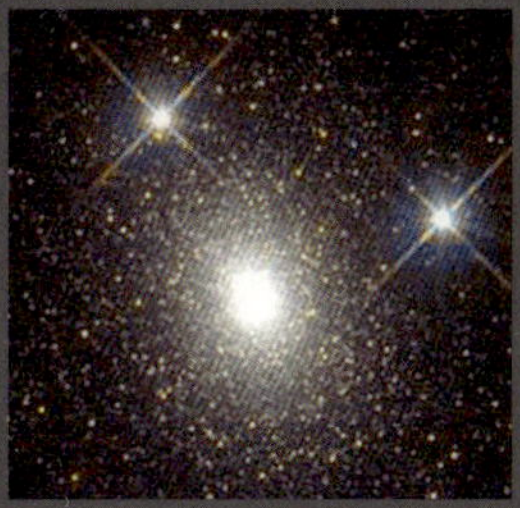
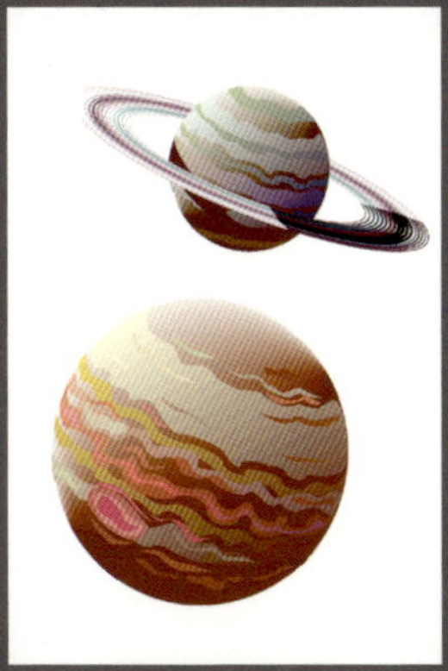
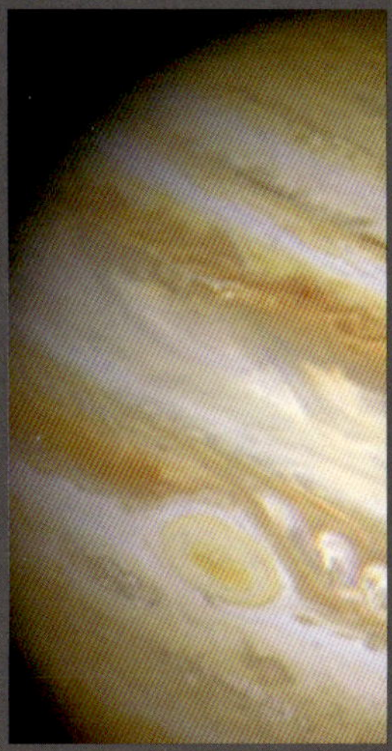

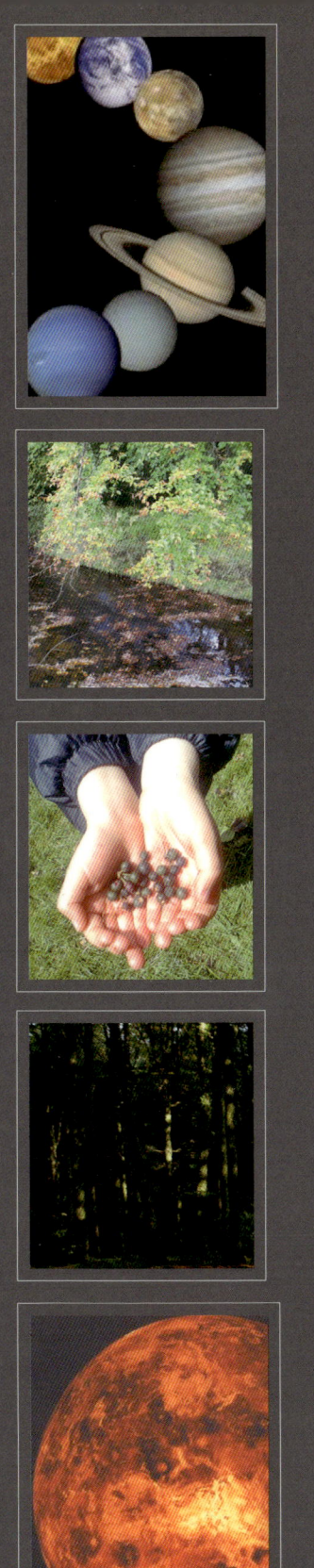

3. Use the code below to fill in the blanks.

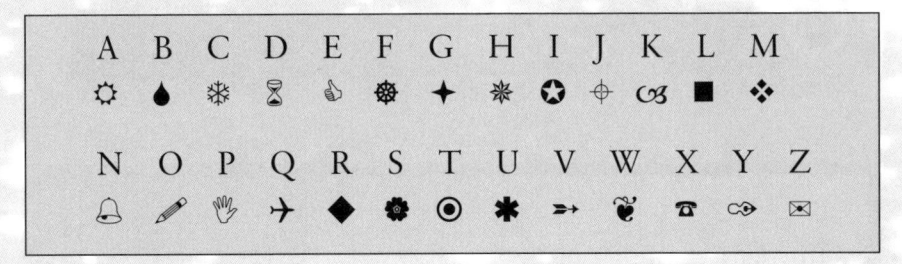

A	B	C	D	E	F	G	H	I	J	K	L	M
☼	●	❄	⌛	👍	❀	◆	✺	★	⊕	✼	■	✦

N	O	P	Q	R	S	T	U	V	W	X	Y	Z
🔔	✏	✋	✈	◆	✿	◉	✵	➔	♥	☎	∞	✉

God has given us:

- **WATER** to **DRINK**
- **LAND** to grow **FOOD** on
- **AIR** to **BREATHE**
- **COAL** and **OIL** to give us **HEAT**

It is our **DUTY** to look after God's Earth and to share all these good things.

We are called to **LOOK AFTER** planet Earth.

8 Silent Stars Speak
The Planets: Venus

Our nearest planet is Venus.

It is closer to the sun than we are, so it is much hotter.

It is the brightest object in the sky after the sun and the moon.

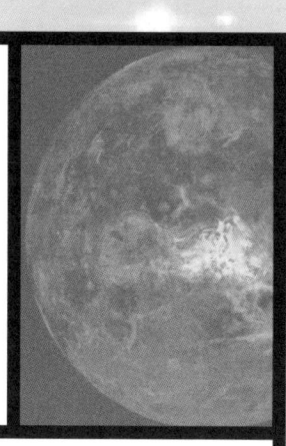

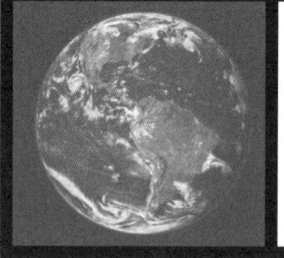

Venus orbits the sun in 225 Earth days.

It takes 243 Earth days to make one Venusian day (the time it takes Venus to rotate once).

1. *Fill in the blanks after reading the boxes above.*

Think! Is a year on Venus shorter or longer than a year on Earth? _____

Think again! Is a day on Venus shorter or longer than a day on Earth? _____

Do you think that Venus rotates faster or slower than Earth? _____

2. Fill in the blanks.

Earth times and Venus times are quite different, and God, who created time, is outside time altogether.

That's why the Bible is able to say, 'A _____ _____ in your sight are like a day that has just gone by, or like a watch in the night' (Psalm 90:4).

Sometimes Venus gets between us and the sun. Then we can see it in broad daylight crossing the surface of the sun.

(WARNING: Never look directly at the sun. It can blind you.)

3. Colour me and the sun.

One Tuesday morning on 4 May 2004, I watched Venus cross the sun by holding binoculars over my shoulder and focusing the sun on a whiteboard.

Slowly Venus bit into the edge of the sun's disc like a giant insect.

Then it crawled across the face of the sun and out at the other side.

It took about four hours to do this, and it won't happen again for another eight years.

After that you will have to wait a further 105 years. It is not to be missed!

VENUS is sometimes called the MORNING STAR because it is sometimes VISIBLE in the EAST just before the SUN RISES.

It HERALDS, or announces, the DAWN.

4. Find and circle in the grid below the words in all capitals from the box above. The words may be up, down, diagonal or backwards.

N	I	G	S	O	D	U	E	F	A	X	B	V	U
A	H	V	E	L	B	I	S	I	V	M	E	T	G
D	E	I	E	I	S	L	J	U	P	I	L	S	E
A	D	Q	S	N	R	C	G	O	B	J	E	A	N
W	K	B	L	H	U	D	A	F	S	S	M	E	O
N	I	H	A	P	O	S	E	U	I	H	G	I	A
B	C	F	E	L	I	M	T	R	O	R	C	K	V
I	O	T	R	A	T	S	G	N	I	N	R	O	M
E	S	U	N	W	N	B	A	K	H	E	N	U	W
L	R	G	U	B	Q	H	E	R	A	L	D	S	I

36

5. *Fill in the blanks.*

Look up Revelation 22:16 and write the last thing that Jesus calls Himself at the end of this verse:

'I am the _____.'

Jesus calls Himself this because He is coming again and will bring His Kingdom with Him. So don't miss getting ready for that!

6. *Follow the instructions.*

- Draw a sun in the middle of the box below.
- Draw Earth and Venus rotating around the sun. *(Remember to make them smaller than the sun. Venus should be the closest to the sun.)*
- Colour the sun yellow, Earth blue and Venus orange.

9 Silent Stars Speak
The Solar System

Other planets that make up our Solar System include Jupiter, Saturn and Mars.

The rest are too small to see with the naked eye.

They are named after Roman gods, but they are not to be worshipped as gods.

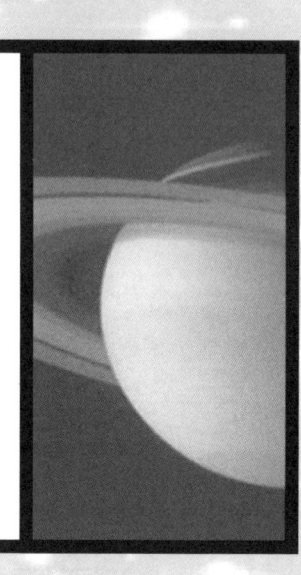

1. *Look up 2 Kings 23:5.*

In this verse, King Josiah does away with the worship of quite a few things in the heavens. Write down as many as you can find:

- _____
- _____
- _____
- _____

2. Write the correct answer on each blank below from the words in the box.

| Shield | fortune | moon |
| Righteousness | Creator | wings |

God our _____ alone is worthy of worship.

The sun, _____ and stars are only created things.

They cannot tell your _____, as some people believe.

Instead, for those who honour God, the 'sun of _____' will rise with healing in its _____. (Malachi 4:2)

'The LORD our God is a sun and _____.' (Psalm 84:11)

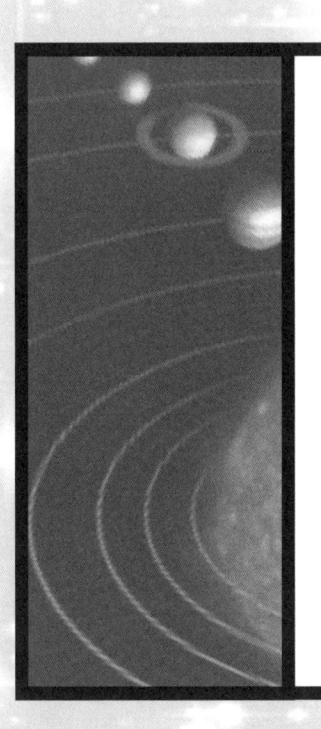

Even so, each planet is wonderful to see. Each is a different size, colour and design.

Although they are all moving, their journey around the sun is so perfect that we know exactly where they are every minute of the day and night.

If they wandered off into deep space, they would be burned up, but God has them all under His control, and they do His will.

You and I have been given freedom to choose God's path or to go our own way.

Unlike the planets, we can wander off course. Then we have to say sorry and come back because Jesus wants to be at the centre of our Solar System.

3. Colour in Saturn and its moons as well as the facts about Saturn's size.

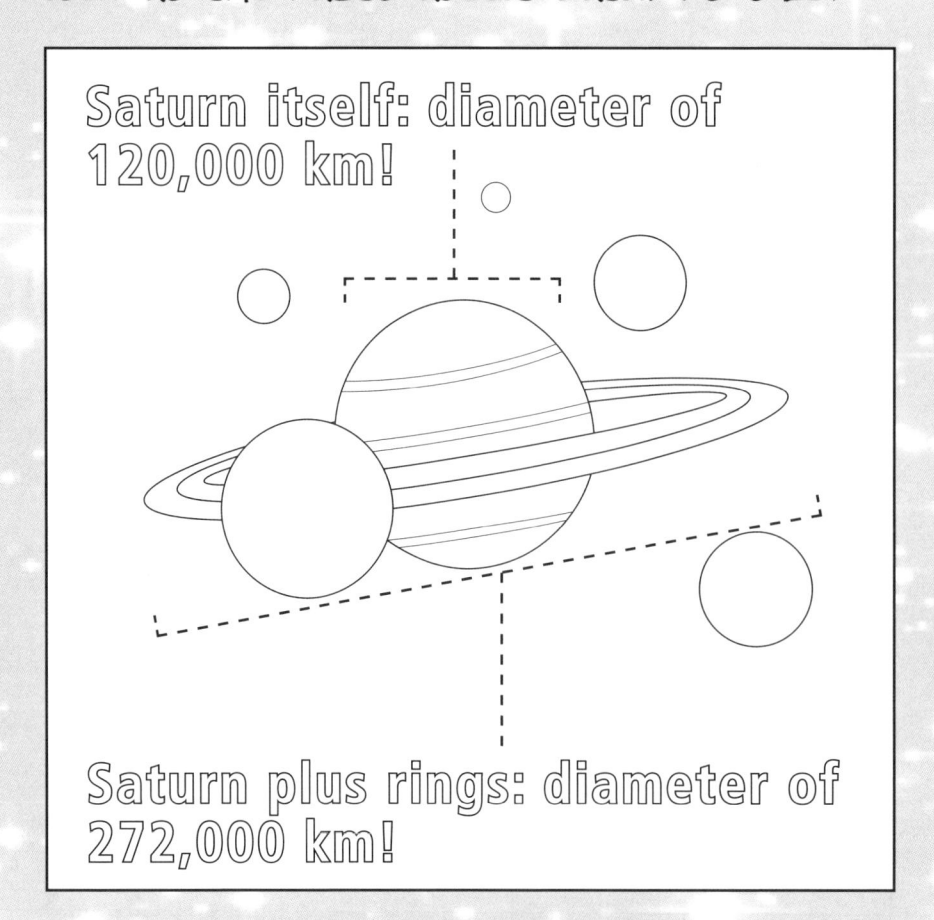

Saturn itself: diameter of 120,000 km!

Saturn plus rings: diameter of 272,000 km!

4. Complete the crossword puzzle using the clues.

DOWN

1. God is called the sun of _____.

5. We don't need to worry about the planets burning up because God has them under His _____.

6. We live in the Solar _____.

ACROSS

2. Our planets are named after the Roman _____.

3. Saturn has many of these orbiting around it.

4. This king in the Bible did away with the worship of the sun, moon and stars.

10 Silent Stars Speak
Comets and Shooting Stars

You will have seen white lines drawn in the blue sky by AEROPLANES.

They are called VAPOUR trails.

COMETS are made of large, ICY chunks of WATER and DUST and come from deep SPACE.

They make long vapour TRAILS when they draw near the sun.

1. Find and circle in the grid below the words in all capitals in the box above. The words may be up, down, diagonal or backwards.

Z	O	G	Y	B	T	I	W	S	A	U	R	S	U
D	V	A	P	O	U	R	L	N	I	P	H	L	D
P	L	C	G	D	R	J	E	C	F	E	W	I	O
I	A	O	S	E	N	A	L	P	O	R	E	A	I
C	R	I	P	H	E	O	B	Q	T	M	C	R	E
Y	E	W	A	T	E	R	I	S	A	L	E	T	S
T	A	J	C	B	F	M	U	I	E	H	O	T	Q
M	R	E	E	U	S	D	U	P	K	N	C	W	S

2. Use the code below to fill in the numbers needed to complete the sentences.

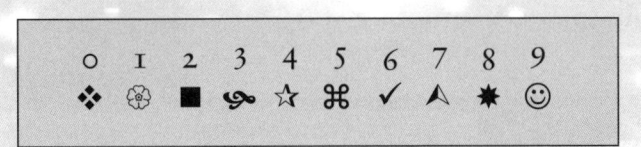

0	1	2	3	4	5	6	7	8	9
❖	❀	■	∾	☆	⌘	✓	⋏	✸	☺

In March ___ ___ ___ ___ a wonderful comet appeared
    ❀ ☺ ☺ ⋏

in the sky. Its name was Hale-Bopp.

It had a bright vapour trail ___ ___ kilometres long.
                              ☆   ❖

Hale-Bopp was last seen at the time of Abraham

because it took ___, ___ ___ ___ years to orbit the sun.
                 ☆   ❖ ■ ✓

Apparently the time varies with each orbit. Its next

orbit will take ___, ___ ___ ___ years. (You can work
                 ■   ∾ ✸ ❖

out when we will see it again!)

Another smaller comet, called Halley's Comet, appears

every ___ ___ years.
      ⋏   ✓

It will be seen again in the year ___ ___ ___ ___.
                                   ■ ❖ ✓ ❀

Its vapour trail is only ___ kilometres long.
                         ✸

When a comet enters our atmosphere, bits of it break up and burn up to create shooting stars.

These shoot across the heavens at great speed and are a wonderful sight.

But only for a moment. Then they are lost forever.

Jude, the brother of Jesus, mentions 'wandering stars'.

They have no direction and disappear into the blackest night.

He says bad people are like that. So be warned.

3. Find Jude 13 and write it out.
   Circle the phrase that describes the way bad people are like wandering stars or comets. Colour in the comets.

They are _____

11 Silent Stars Speak
Eclipse of the Sun

Sometimes the moon gets between Earth and the sun. Then it can black out part, or all, of the sun. We call it an eclipse.

PARTIAL ECLIPSE   TOTAL ECLIPSE

There was a total eclipse in March 2006, and the sun's light was hidden for four minutes in the middle of the day. The temperature dropped, the birds flew back to their nests, the animals got confused and there was an eerie silence.

How can the moon cover the sun when the sun is 400 times as big?

The answer is that the sun is 400 times further away from us, so it looks the same size as the moon.

1. *Try it! Hold a 2p coin to your eye and see if you can cover the clock face, or a similar object, on the opposite side of the room.*

2. Let's do some investigating! Follow instructions and give the right answers.

The Mystery at Jesus' Death

- Look up and read Matthew 27:38–46. When Jesus was crucified, there was what over all of Earth?
  _____

- Some people say that this was a **loatt** _____ eclipse of the sun, but we know better. (Unscramble the letters for the right answer.)

- Look at verse 45 again. How many hours did this 'eclipse' last? _____ (Clue: Today we would say it lasted from midday until three o'clock.)

- A natural eclipse, on the other hand, lasts at the most 7 **uemtsni** _____. (Unscramble the letters for the right answer.)

A	B	C	D	E	F	G	H	I	J	K	L	M
1	2	3	4	5	6	7	8	9	10	11	12	13

N	O	P	Q	R	S	T	U	V	W	X	Y	Z
14	15	16	17	18	19	20	21	22	23	24	25	26

- Use the code above to discover the real reason why this darkness happened:

  Jesus, the ___ ___ ___ ___ ___ of the world, was
               12 9 7 8 20

  suffering and dying for our ___ ___ ___ ___ , and
                               19 9 14 19

  the ___ ___ ___ stopped shining.
        19 21 14

- Now look up Job 9:7. What does the Bible say God does to the sun?

  _____

  _____

3. Circle the right answer to the questions.

- When the moon completely covers the sun, we call it a _____ eclipse.
  A. partial   B. total

- An eclipse usually lasts a few _____.
  A. hours   B. minutes

- The darkness at Jesus' death lasted _____ hours.
  A. three   B. five

- When Jesus was crucified, the _____ stopped shining.
  A. moon   B. sun

- While Jesus was dying for our _____, darkness covered Earth.
  A. light   B. sins

4. Find and circle in the grid the correct answers to the questions above. They may be up, down or across.

Q	E	E	T	Y	P	L	E	O	S
A	U	W	O	S	A	U	E	X	C
R	I	H	T	L	T	R	R	E	A
T	N	C	A	G	I	M	H	U	I
S	U	N	L	R	B	E	T	N	S
M	A	E	O	S	I	O	G	A	P
D	M	I	N	U	T	E	S	H	U
H	F	B	E	R	D	L	T	V	N
O	T	K	H	S	I	N	S	E	J

12 Silent Stars Speak
The Christmas Star

This is surely the most exciting star of all.

The wise men followed the star from East to West, all the way to Bethlehem.

1. *Look up Matthew 2:9 and write on the blank where the star took the wise men to.*

It stopped right over _____.

Some astronomers believe the star the wise men followed was Halley's Comet.

Chinese astronomers at the time described it in great detail.

First seen in the reign of Emperor Yuan-Yen on 25 August 12 BC, it was observed for 63 days before disappearing in a northerly direction.

But if Jesus was born in approximately 6 BC, as most scholars believe, it is six years too early.

Others say it was a meeting of the planets Jupiter and Saturn.

Very rarely, two planets draw so close to each other that they produce one brilliant light. This is called a conjunction.

The Astronomer Royal Johannes Kepler noticed this on 17 December 1603.

He remembered that the Jewish astrologers had said that this would be a sign of the coming Messiah.

Today, we can turn back the cosmic clock in a planetarium, and we find that Jupiter and Saturn did indeed meet in 7 BC just when the wise men were supposed to have set out on their long journey.

In fact, these two planets met three times in that year on 29 May, 3 October and 4 December.

However, other people prefer to believe that this was a special star created for a very special occasion and that when its work was done it disappeared as mysteriously as it had come.

2. Complete the crossword.

DOWN

1. Some people think the Christmas star could have been Halley's _____.

3. Jewish astrologers thought that the conjunction of Jupiter and Saturn would mean the coming of this person.

5. One of the months in which Jupiter and Saturn met in 7 BC was _____.

6. Astronomers in this country saw Halley's Comet a few years before Jesus was born.

8. The planet with many rings around it

ACROSS

2. This astronomer observed the meeting of Jupiter and Saturn.

4. The wise men came from this direction.

7. The meeting of two planets is called this.

9. The largest planet in our Solar System

3. Colour in the verse and picture of the wise men following the star.

When they saw the star, they were overjoyed.
-Matthew 2:10

Answers to Activities

1 Silent Stars Speak
In the Beginning

The night was cold and crystal clear. The sky was ablaze with stars.

What were they saying? What were they singing? Psalm 19 gives the answer.

1. Unscramble the letters to find out what Psalm 19:1 says.

The **heavens** declare the **glory** of God.
   NAHVESE   LYROG

Have you ever stepped out of doors on a dark, clear night and gazed at the stars?

If it's dark enough and away from the street lights' glare, you can see hundreds of them.

The sky is not empty at all. It is full of little lights besides stars.

2. Name the following things that fill the sky.

- planet
- comet
- shooting star
- satellite

All of these are hanging in space.

Some planets are bigger than our sun, but they are so far away they look like tiny specks.

Where did all these lights come from?

Some people say there was a BIG BANG, like a giant firework exploding, and stars were shot out into space.

The Bible says God made them. He flung them into space.

3. Use the code below to complete the sentence.

A	B	C	D	E	F	G	H	I	J	K	L	M
1	2	3	4	5	6	7	8	9	10	11	12	13

N	O	P	Q	R	S	T	U	V	W	X	Y	Z
14	15	16	17	18	19	20	21	22	23	24	25	26

God is a l l   p o w e r f u l
       1 12 12 16 15 23 5 18 6 21 12

4. Unscramble the letters using Genesis 1:14, 18.

God said, 'Let there be **lights** in the sky.'
                        TLSHIG

And God saw that it was **good**.
                         OGDO

God made the earth and the sky, and then He filled the sky with lights.

5. Read Genesis 1:14-16. Complete the crossword puzzle using what you read and the clues.

DOWN

1. The stars were created to help us figure these out; each of these are made up of 365 days.
2. The lesser light
3. The stars were created to give light on this planet.

ACROSS

4, 5. God created lights to divide or separate the ____ from the ____.
6. One of the functions of stars is to help us tell the four of these.

Crossword:
- 4 across: day
- 1 down: year
- 2 down: moon
- 3 down: earth
- 6 across: seasons
- 5 across: night

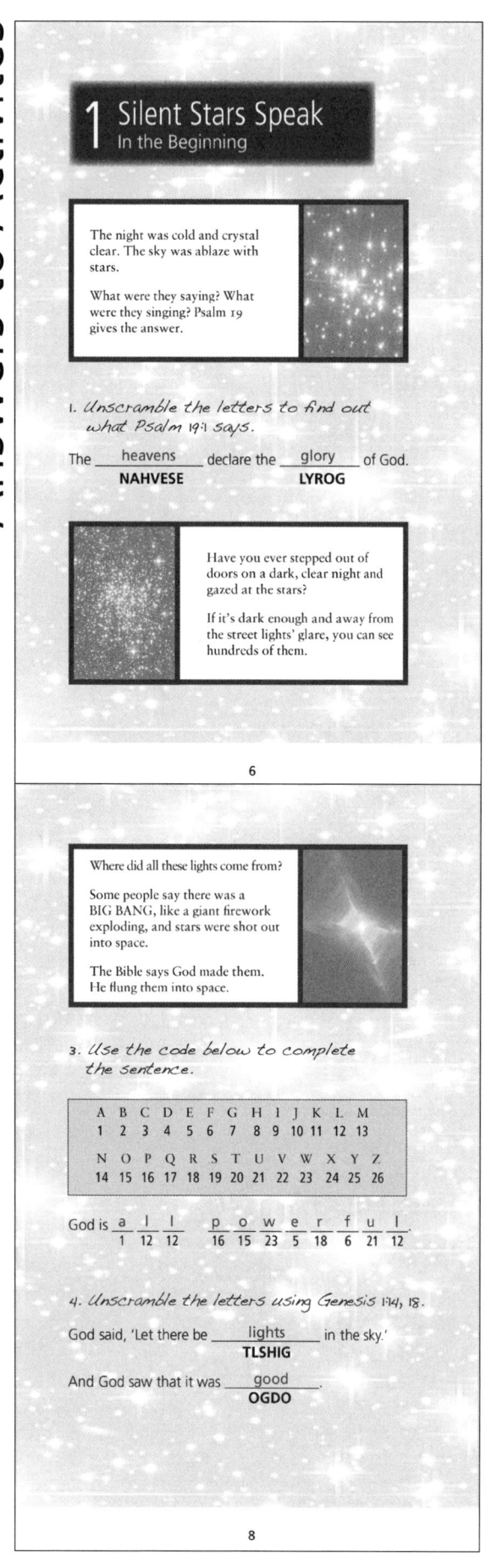

54

2 Silent Stars Speak
Each One is Special

1. Read Psalm 147:4. What two things beginning with the letter 'n' does God know about the stars?

   Their n <u>umber</u> and their n <u>ames</u>

2. Fill in the blanks with the opposite of each word in brackets.

   Each star is <u>different</u> (the same).
   Some are <u>near</u> (far).
   Some are <u>far</u> (near).
   Some are <u>black</u> (white).
   Some are blue, red or orange.
   Some are <u>big</u> (small).
   Some are <u>smaller</u> (bigger).
   Some are very <u>hot</u> (cold).
   Some are not.

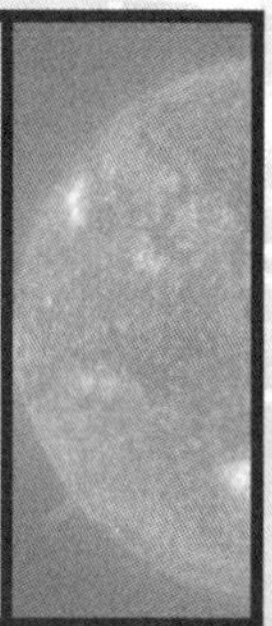

Our nearest STAR is the sun. In fact, all stars are suns, and they all give out light and HEAT.

The sun is 400 times further away from us than the MOON.

So if you climbed a sunbeam, it would take you three THOUSAND six hundred years to get there.

The sun is also 400 times BIGGER than the moon. So from Earth they both look the same SIZE.

God has given us the sun to give us LIGHT and WARMTH.

All our life and ENERGY come from the sun.

If we were any nearer to the sun, we would BURN up. If we were any further away from the sun, we would freeze.

We are just the right DISTANCE away.

God is GOOD.

3. Find all the words in CAPITALS in the boxes above and write them here:
   <u>star, heat, moon, thousand, bigger, size, light, warmth, energy, burn, distance, good</u>

---

4. Look for the words in capitals you wrote down on the previous page in the letter grid below and colour them in. The words may be up, down, diagonal or backwards.

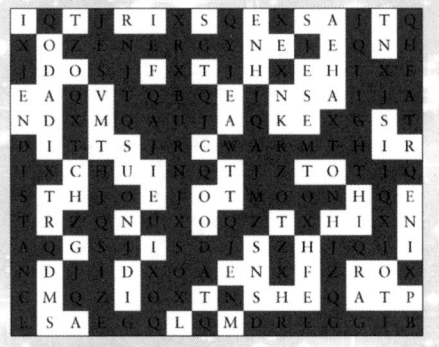

5. Colour in all boxes with the letters J, Q, X and Z in the letter grid.

6. Write the letters left over on the blanks below from left to right to read a Bible verse about the sun.

   <u>It rises at one end of the heavens and makes its circuit to the other; nothing is hidden from its heat.</u>

   <u>Psalm</u> 19:6

Our nearest neighbour in the sky is the moon.

It's very near compared to the stars. In fact, men have visited the moon and walked on its surface.

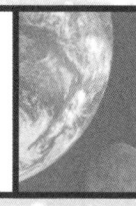

7. Use the code below to complete the sentences.

If you could walk up a <u>moonbeam</u> at the same rate that you walk to school, you could get there in just <u>nine</u> years.

The moon has no light of its own, but it reflects the <u>sunlight</u> like a mirror.

Neil Armstrong was the first man to step onto the moon. When he did so, he said: 'That's one small step for man, one giant leap for mankind.'

3 Silent Stars Speak
N.S.E.W.

1. *Unscramble the letters to spell one of the four directions—North, South, East or West.*

The sun rises in the ___east___.
SATE

If you look in the direction of the sunrise, you are looking East.

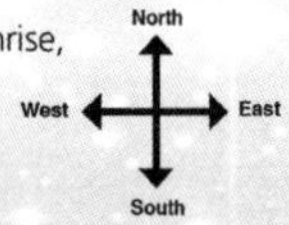

The sun sets in the ___west___.
TWSE
which is on the opposite side of the sky.

If your house faces East and West, you can watch the sun rise in the morning and then set in the evening.

At midday the sun is halfway between the East and West, and we call that ___south___ (unless you live in Australia!). **TOSUH**

Opposite the South is the ___north___.
ORHTN

We can divide the sky up into four quarters like a sponge cake, and we call the quarters the N.S.E.W. parts of the sky.

Of course, the sun doesn't really rise and set at all. It stays where it is.

It's our little world that spins round like a top toward the sun.

It spins at a thousand miles an hour from West to East.

You can't feel it spinning because the air spins with it.

So in the morning, one side of the world faces the sun and in the evening, the other side of the world faces the sun.

So every hour of the day, people are waking up to a new day and there is always somebody praising God.

2. *Answer the following questions:*

On what side of the earth are you right now—the dark or the light side? ___Answers will vary.___

On what side of the earth are you when you sleep at night? ___the dark side___

What would somebody on the other side of the world be doing when you are getting ready to go to bed?
___getting up from bed___

---

3. *Read this poem out loud:*

> Across each continent and island
> As dawn leads on another day,
> The voice of prayer is never silent,
> Nor dies the sound of praise away.
> –from 'The day thou gavest'
> by John Ellerton

5. *According to this poem, what are people doing somewhere on earth all the time?*
___praising the Lord___

4. *Find Psalm 113:3 and fill in the missing blanks from it:*

'From the rising of the ___sun___ to the place where it sets, the name of the ___Lord___ is to be praised.'

---

5. *Follow these instructions.*

Put the four directions in order so that the first letter of each reads GOOD n e w s . (For a clue, you will find the words in Luke 2:10).

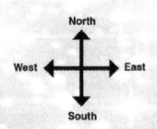

5. *Circle the right answer. The answers are on this activity sheet.*

How fast does the Earth spin each hour?
A. ten miles each hour
B. hundred miles each hour
(C. thousand miles each hour)
D. million miles each hour

In what direction does the Earth spin?
A. North to South
(B. West to East)
C. South to North
D. East to West

In what direction does the sun set?
A. North
B. South
C. East
(D. West)

4 Silent Stars Speak
The Signpost

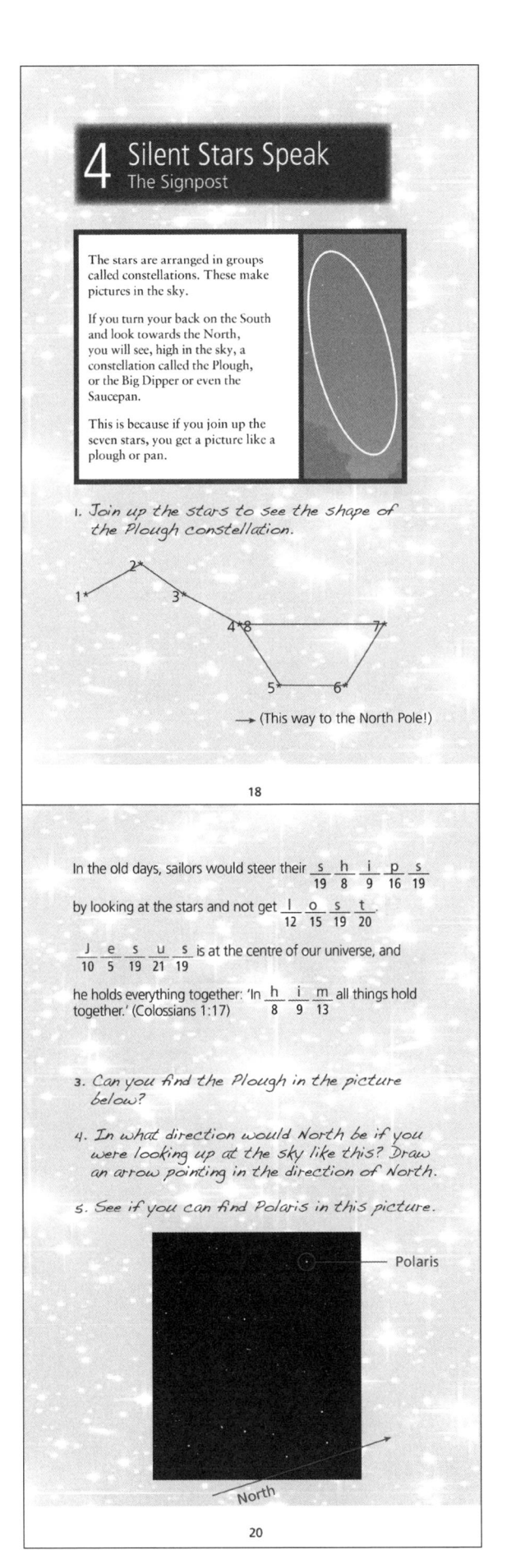

The stars are arranged in groups called constellations. These make pictures in the sky.

If you turn your back on the South and look towards the North, you will see, high in the sky, a constellation called the Plough, or the Big Dipper or even the Saucepan.

This is because if you join up the seven stars, you get a picture like a plough or pan.

1. Join up the stars to see the shape of the Plough constellation.

→ (This way to the North Pole!)

2. Use the code below to complete the sentences.

A	B	C	D	E	F	G	H	I	J	K	L	M
1	2	3	4	5	6	7	8	9	10	11	12	13
N	O	P	Q	R	S	T	U	V	W	X	Y	Z
14	15	16	17	18	19	20	21	22	23	24	25	26

Stars numbers 6 and 7 point to the Pole star called P o l a r i s.
16 15 12 1 18 9 19

Sailors at sea and some b i r d s on migration find their way by this star.
2 9 18 4 19

Over one y e a r, the Plough will revolve full circle
25 5 1 18
around this star, but 6 and 7 will always point to it.

Polaris is the one point in the sky which is fixed so you can always find n o r t h.
14 15 18 20 8

In the old days, sailors would steer their s h i p s
19 8 9 16 19
by looking at the stars and not get l o s t.
12 15 19 20

J e s u s is at the centre of our universe, and
10 5 19 21 19

he holds everything together: 'In h i m all things hold
8 9 13
together.' (Colossians 1:17)

3. Can you find the Plough in the picture below?

4. In what direction would North be if you were looking up at the sky like this? Draw an arrow pointing in the direction of North.

5. See if you can find Polaris in this picture.

Polaris

North

6. Complete the crossword puzzle using the clues.

DOWN
1. Another name for the Plough
3. Sailors used the stars as these so they wouldn't get lost.
4. These people used the stars to find their way at sea.

ACROSS
2. Who is at the centre of our universe?
5. We can use Polaris to find this direction.
6. The Plough revolves around this star.
7. It takes one _____ for the Plough to revolve around the answer to number 6.

1 Saucepan
2 Jesus
4 sailors
5 north
6 Polaris
7 years

2. Find and colour the words of Matthew 19:26 on the word grid. The words may be up, down, diagonal or backwards. Colour only one 'with'.

'With man this is impossible; but with God all things are possible.'

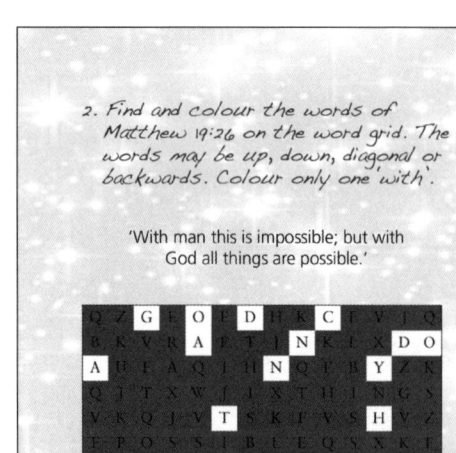

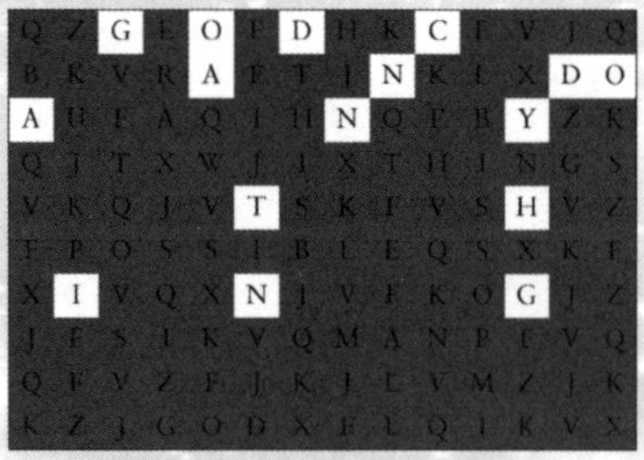

3. Colour in all boxes with the letters F, J, K, Q, V, X and Z.

4. From left to right, write out the letters you see on the blanks below. What do they say?

<u>G</u> <u>o</u> <u>d</u> <u>c</u> <u>a</u> <u>n</u> <u>d</u> <u>o</u>
<u>a</u> <u>n</u> <u>y</u> <u>t</u> <u>h</u> <u>i</u> <u>n</u> <u>g</u>.

24

6 Silent Stars Speak
The Dog Star

I have a little dog. He walks just behind my left heel.

Orion the hunter has a dog too. He walks just behind Orion's left heel.

The dog's eye is the brightest star in the sky. It's called Sirius.

The little dog follows his master right across the sky just as Jesus wants us to follow him.

Sirius •

1. Find out who uses this star and what they call it. On each blank, write the letter that comes alphabetically before the letter under the blank.

<u>S</u> <u>a</u> <u>i</u> <u>l</u> <u>o</u> <u>r</u> <u>s</u> call it the <u>D</u> <u>o</u> <u>g</u>
T B J M P S T   E P H

<u>s</u> <u>t</u> <u>a</u> <u>r</u> and use it to guide them home.
T U B S

26

In fact, Orion has two dogs which follow him across the sky.

One is called Big Dog, and one is called Little Dog.

Big Dog keeps close to his master's heel. Little Dog trots along behind.

Usually all we can see of these dogs is a single star!

2. Fill in the blanks below and on the next page with the rest of the words from the list that will fit.

MAJOR   MINOR   EYE   PROCYON

Another name for the Big Dog star is Canis Ma<u>jo</u>r.

Another name for the Little Dog star is Canis Mi<u>no</u>r.

27

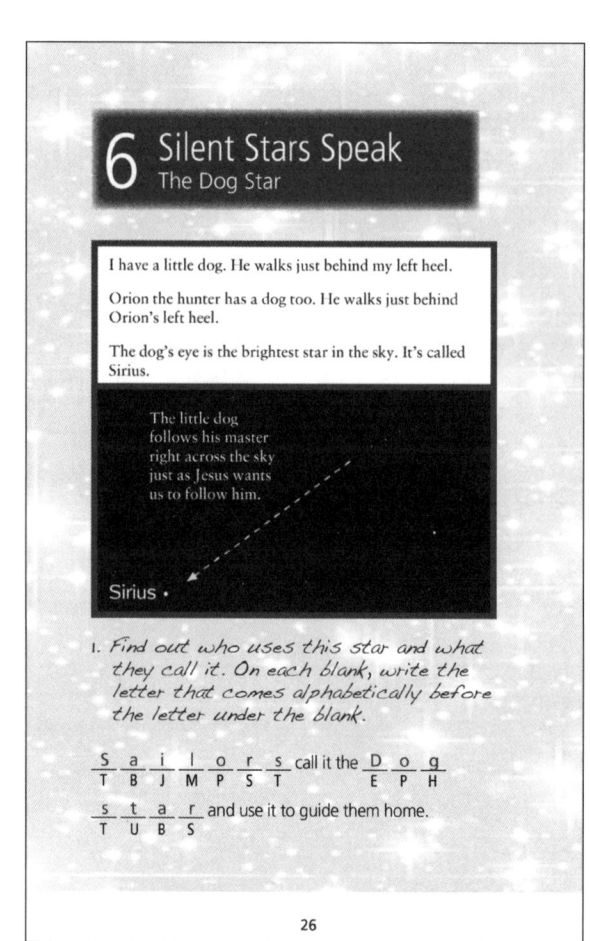

Little Dog's brightest star is called P<u>rocyo</u>n.

The part of Little Dog's body that is the brightest in the sky is the <u>eye</u>.

Betaljeuse, Sirius and Procyon make a bright triangle in the winter sky.

3. Connect the three stars to make a triangle. Then write the name of each star beside the right letter.

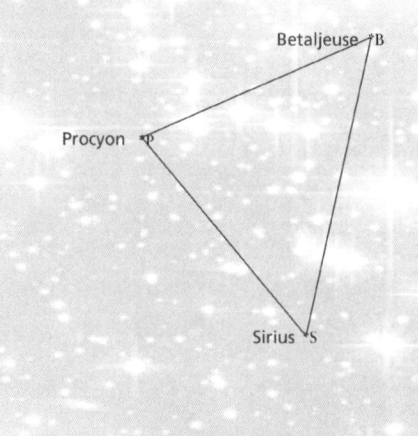

Betaljeuse •B

Procyon •P

Sirius •S

28

58

4. Complete the crossword puzzle using the clues.

DOWN
2. Little Dog's brightest star
4. Another name for the Dog star
5. The part of Little Dog's body that is the brightest

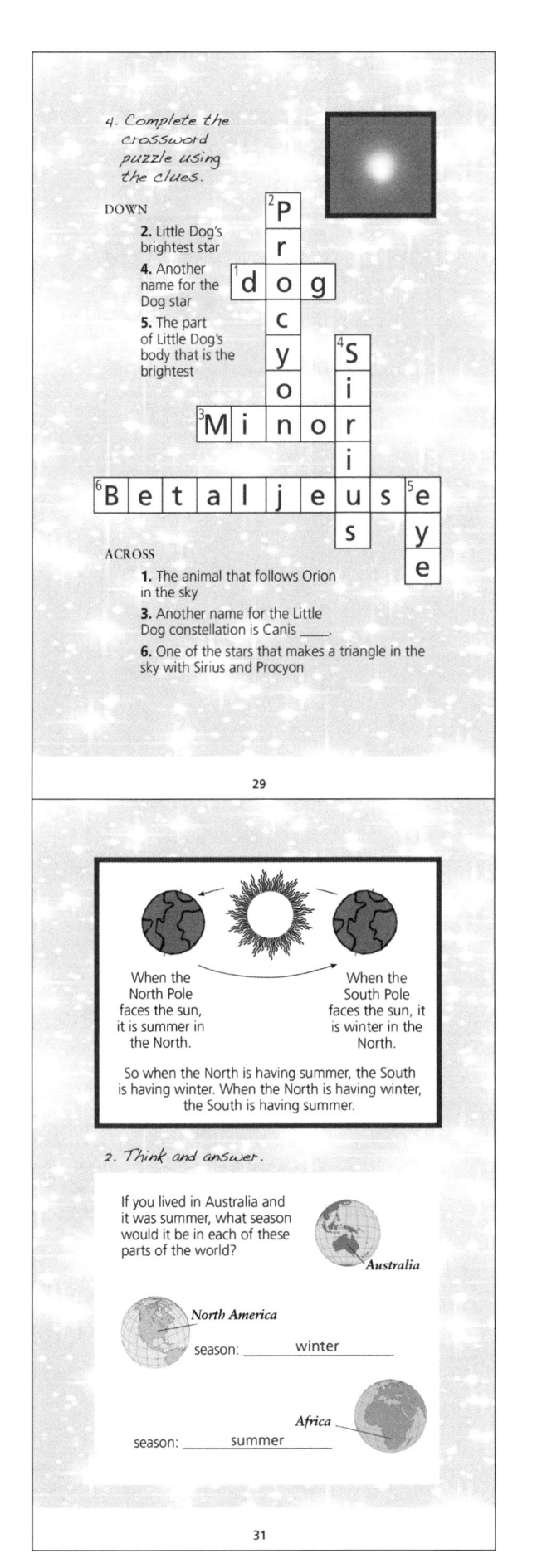

ACROSS
1. The animal that follows Orion in the sky
3. Another name for the Little Dog constellation is Canis ____.
6. One of the stars that makes a triangle in the sky with Sirius and Procyon

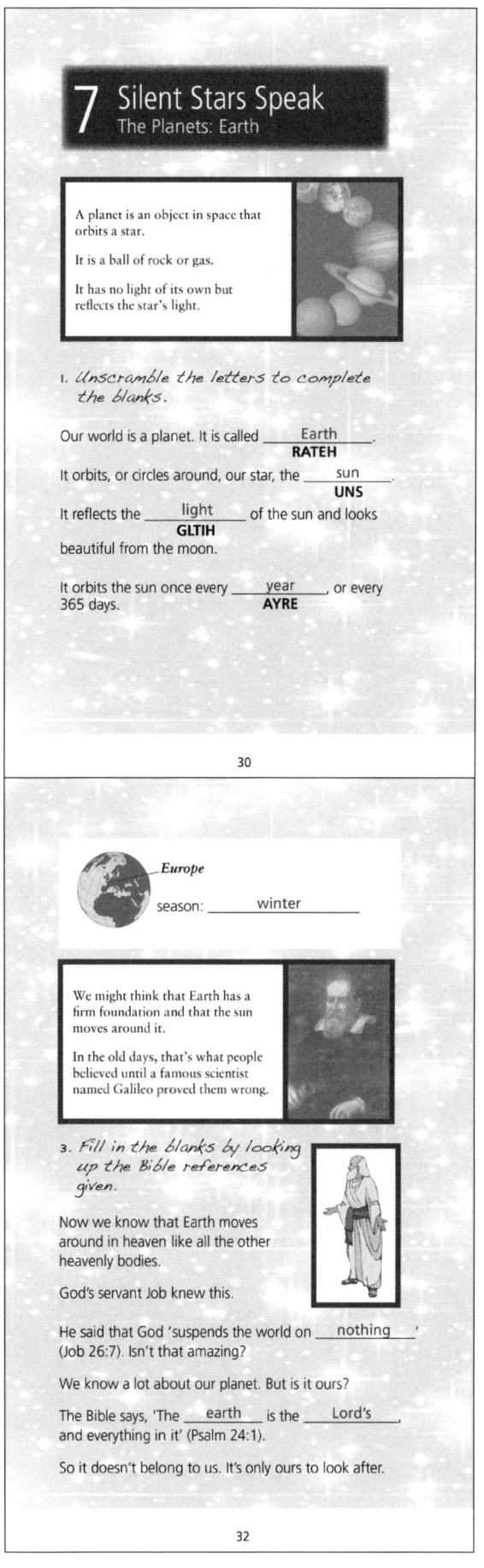

Crossword answers:
- 1 across: dog
- 2 down: Procyon
- 3 across: Minor
- 4 down: Sirius
- 5 down: eye
- 6 across: Betaljeuse

---

7 Silent Stars Speak
The Planets: Earth

A planet is an object in space that orbits a star.

It is a ball of rock or gas.

It has no light of its own but reflects the star's light.

1. Unscramble the letters to complete the blanks.

Our world is a planet. It is called **Earth** (RATEH).

It orbits, or circles around, our star, the **sun** (UNS).

It reflects the **light** (GLTIH) of the sun and looks beautiful from the moon.

It orbits the sun once every **year** (AYRE), or every 365 days.

When the North Pole faces the sun, it is summer in the North.

When the South Pole faces the sun, it is winter in the North.

So when the North is having summer, the South is having winter. When the North is having winter, the South is having summer.

2. Think and answer.

If you lived in Australia and it was summer, what season would it be in each of these parts of the world?

North America season: **winter**

Africa season: **summer**

Europe season: **winter**

We might think that Earth has a firm foundation and that the sun moves around it.

In the old days, that's what people believed until a famous scientist named Galileo proved them wrong.

3. Fill in the blanks by looking up the Bible references given.

Now we know that Earth moves around in heaven like all the other heavenly bodies.

God's servant Job knew this.

He said that God 'suspends the world on **nothing**' (Job 26:7). Isn't that amazing?

We know a lot about our planet. But is it ours?

The Bible says, 'The **earth** is the **Lord's** and everything in it' (Psalm 24:1).

So it doesn't belong to us. It's only ours to look after.

3. Use the code below to fill in the blanks.

God has given us:

- <u>w a t e r</u> to <u>d r i n k</u>

- <u>l a n d</u> to grow <u>f o o d</u> on

- <u>a i r</u> to <u>b r e a t h e</u>

- <u>c o a l</u> and <u>o i l</u> to give us <u>h e a t</u>

It is our <u>d u t y</u> to look after God's Earth and to share all these good things.

We are called to <u>l o o k</u> <u>a f t e r</u> planet Earth.

---

8 Silent Stars Speak
The Planets: Venus

Our nearest planet is Venus.

It is closer to the sun than we are, so it is much hotter.

It is the brightest object in the sky after the sun and the moon.

Venus orbits the sun in 225 Earth days.

It takes 243 Earth days to make one Venusian day (the time it takes Venus to rotate once).

1. Fill in the blanks after reading the boxes above.

Think! Is a year on Venus shorter or longer than a year on Earth? __shorter__

Think again! Is a day on Venus shorter or longer than a day on Earth? __longer__

Do you think that Venus rotates faster or slower than Earth? __slower__

---

2. Fill in the blanks.

Earth times and Venus times are quite different, and God, who created time, is outside time altogether.

That's why the Bible is able to say, 'A __thousand years__ in your sight are like a day that has just gone by, or like a watch in the night' (Psalm 90:4).

Sometimes Venus gets between us and the sun. Then we can see it in broad daylight crossing the surface of the sun.

(WARNING: Never look directly at the sun. It can blind you.)

One Tuesday morning on 4 May 2004, I watched Venus cross the sun by holding binoculars over my shoulder and focusing the sun on a whiteboard.

Slowly Venus bit into the edge of the sun's disc like a giant insect.

Then it crawled across the face of the sun and out at the other side.

It took about four hours to do this, and it won't happen again for another eight years.

After that you will have to wait a further 105 years. It is not to be missed!

3. Colour me and the sun.

VENUS is sometimes called the MORNING STAR because it is sometimes VISIBLE in the EAST just before the SUN RISES.

It HERALDS, or announces, the DAWN.

4. Find and circle in the grid below the words in all capitals from the box above. The words may be up, down, diagonal or backwards.

N	I	G	S	O	D	U	E	F	A	X	B	V	U
A	H	V	E	L	B	I	S	I	V	M	E	T	G
D	E	I	E	I	S	L	J	U	P	I	L	S	E
A	D	Q	S	N	R	C	G	O	B	J	E	A	N
W	K	B	L	H	U	D	A	F	S	S	M	E	O
N	I	H	A	P	O	S	E	U	I	H	G	I	A
B	C	F	E	L	I	M	T	R	O	R	C	K	V
I	O	T	R	A	T	S	G	N	I	N	R	O	M
E	S	U	N	W	N	B	A	K	H	E	N	U	W
L	R	G	U	B	Q	H	E	R	A	L	D	S	I

5. Fill in the blanks.

Look up Revelation 22:16 and write the last thing that Jesus calls Himself at the end of this verse:

'I am the __bright morning star__.'
(Answers may vary, depending on the Bible version used.)
Jesus calls Himself this because He is coming again and will bring His Kingdom with Him. So don't miss getting ready for that!

6. Follow the instructions.

- Draw a sun in the middle of the box below.
- Draw Earth and Venus rotating around the sun. *(Remember to make them smaller than the sun. Venus should be the closest to the sun.)*
- Colour the sun yellow, Earth blue and Venus orange.

Check if directions above are followed.

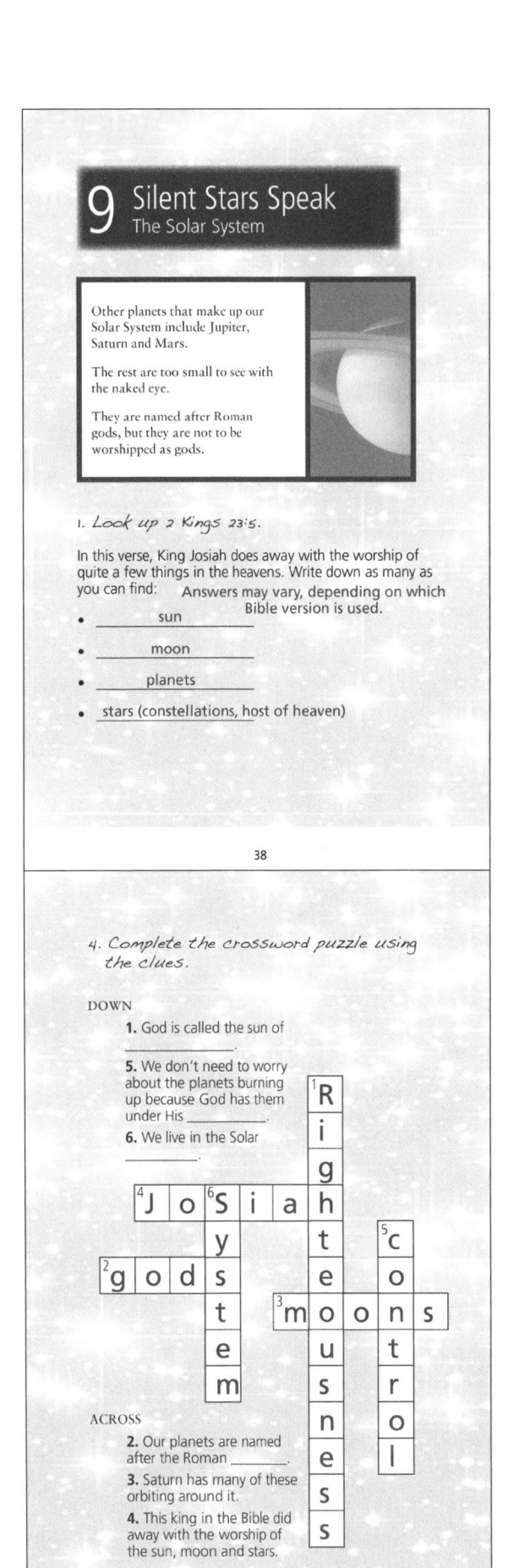

9 Silent Stars Speak
The Solar System

Other planets that make up our Solar System include Jupiter, Saturn and Mars.

The rest are too small to see with the naked eye.

They are named after Roman gods, but they are not to be worshipped as gods.

1. Look up 2 Kings 23:5.

In this verse, King Josiah does away with the worship of quite a few things in the heavens. Write down as many as you can find: Answers may vary, depending on which Bible version is used.

- __sun__
- __moon__
- __planets__
- __stars__ (constellations, host of heaven)

---

2. Write the correct answer on each blank below from the words in the box.

| Shield | fortune | moon |
| Righteousness | Creator | wings |

God our __Creator__ alone is worthy of worship.

The sun, __moon__ and stars are only created things.

They cannot tell your __fortune__, as some people believe.

Instead, for those who honour God, the 'sun of __Righteousness__' will rise with healing in its __wings__. (Malachi 4:2)

'The LORD our God is a sun and __Shield__.' (Psalm 84:11)

Even so, each planet is wonderful to see. Each is a different size, colour and design.

Although they are all moving, their journey around the sun is so perfect that we know exactly where they are every minute of the day and night.

If they wandered off into deep space, they would be burned up, but God has them all under His control, and they do His will.

---

4. Complete the crossword puzzle using the clues.

DOWN
1. God is called the sun of _____
5. We don't need to worry about the planets burning up because God has them under His _____.
6. We live in the Solar _____.

ACROSS
2. Our planets are named after the Roman _____.
3. Saturn has many of these orbiting around it.
4. This king in the Bible did away with the worship of the sun, moon and stars.

Crossword answers:
1 Down: Righteousness
5 Down: control
6 Down: system
2 Across: gods
3 Across: moons
4 Across: Josiah

10 Silent Stars Speak
Comets and Shooting Stars

You will have seen white lines drawn in the blue sky by AEROPLANES.

They are called VAPOUR trails.

COMETS are made of large, ICY chunks of WATER and DUST and come from deep SPACE.

They make long vapour TRAILS when they draw near the sun.

1. Find and circle in the grid below the words in all capitals in the box above. The words may be up, down, diagonal or backwards.

```
Z O G Y B T I W S A U R S U
D V A P O U R L N I P H L D
P L C G D R J E C F E W I O
I A O S E N A L P O R E A I
C R I P H E O B Q T M C R E
Y E W A T E R S A L E T S
T A J C B F M U T E H O T Q
M R E E U S D U P K N C W S
```

2. Use the code below to fill in the numbers needed to complete the sentences.

0	1	2	3	4	5	6	7	8	9
✧	⊕	■	✎	☆	⌘	✓	▲	✱	☉

In March __1__ __9__ __9__ __7__ a wonderful comet appeared in the sky. Its name was Hale-Bopp.

It had a bright vapour trail __4__ __0__ kilometres long.

Hale-Bopp was last seen at the time of Abraham because it took __4__ __0__ __2__ __6__ years to orbit the sun.

Apparently the time varies with each orbit. Its next orbit will take __2__ __3__ __8__ __0__ years. (You can work out when we will see it again!)

Another smaller comet, called Halley's Comet, appears every __7__ __6__ years.

It will be seen again in the year __2__ __0__ __6__ __1__.

Its vapour trail is only __8__ kilometres long.

3. Find Jude 13 and write it out. Circle the phrase that describes the way bad people are like wandering stars or comets. Colour in the comets.

They are ___wild waves of___ ___the sea, foaming up___ ___their shame; (wandering)___ ___(stars) for whom blackest___ ___darkness has been reserved___ ___forever.___

2. Let's do some investigating! Follow instructions and give the right answers.

The Mystery at Jesus' Death

- Look up and read Matthew 27:38–46. When Jesus was crucified, there was what over all of Earth? ___darkness___

- Some people say that this was a **loatt** ___total___ eclipse of the sun, but we know better. (Unscramble the letters for the right answer.)

- Look at verse 45 again. How many hours did this 'eclipse' last? ___3 hours___ (Clue: Today we would say it lasted from midday until three o'clock.)

- A natural eclipse, on the other hand, lasts at the most 7 **uemtsni** ___3 minutes___. (Unscramble the letters for the right answer.)